Alfred J. Hough

Solomon's Song Re-Sung, and Other Poems

Alfred J. Hough

Solomon's Song Re-Sung, and Other Poems

ISBN/EAN: 9783337318550

Printed in Europe, USA, Canada, Australia, Japan

Cover: Foto ©Thomas Meinert / pixelio.de

More available books at **www.hansebooks.com**

SOLOMON'S SONG RE-SUNG,

AND

OTHER POEMS.

BY

ALFRED J. HOUGH,
MINISTER OF THE M. E. CHURCH.

—◆—

BOSTON:
PUBLISHED FOR THE AUTHOR.
J. BENT AND COMPANY.
1874.

Entered, according to Act of Congress, in the year 1874,
By REV. ALFRED J. HOUGH,
In the Office of the Librarian of Congress, at Washington.

Stereotyped and printed by Rand, Avery, & Co., Boston.

THE author has endeavored, in the remoulding of Solomon's Song, to sing for Jesus, and to produce such a volume as shall make an acceptable addition to the collections of sacred melodies used in the various services of the Church of Christ.

CONTENTS.

SOLOMON'S SONG RE-SUNG.

	PAGE.
The Song of Songs	9
The Kiss of Jesus	11
The Love of Jesus	12
The Name of Jesus	13
Man condemned by Angels	14
Hasting to find Jesus	15
Guests of the King	16
Rejoicing in Jesus	17
Remembering Jesus	18
The Lord our Righteousness	20
Bearing Reproach for Jesus	21
Denying Self for Others. — The Pastor	22
The Pastor's Confession	23
Where feedest Thou?	24
The Noontide Rest	25
Darkness	28
Forsaking Jesus	29
Follow the Good	30
The Children for Jesus. — Future Triumphs	31
Strength and Beauty of the Church	32
Love's Offering	33
The Preciousness of Jesus	34
Faithfulness. — The Great Restorative	35
Changed	36
The Church in the World	37
The House of God. — The Loveliness of Jesus	38
Christ Pre-eminent	39
Under the Cross	40
Holy Living	41
Home at Last	42
Love's Banner	43

CONTENTS.

	PAGE
Over-Joy	44
Divine Support and Protection	46
Behold, He cometh!	48
Sorrow Past. — Following Jesus	50
Tokens of Love	51
A Time of Joy	52
Sabbath-School Revival. — Little Sins	54
In the Rock I'm hiding	55
The Desire of Jesus. — Mine and His	57
Christ and his Lilies	58
Waiting for the Dawn	59
Seeking Rest in Seclusion	61
Found	62
Seeking Rest in the World	63
The Coming of Love	64
The King's Army	66
Watchfulness. — Holding on to Jesus	67
Spotless	68
Waiting near the Cross	69
Look away to Jesus. — The Power of one Pure Heart	70
The Acceptable Offering	71
The Work of Love	72
The Enclosed Garden	73
The Plants and Pleasant Fruits	74
The Fountain	75
Blow, Spirit, Blow! — Welcome to Jesus	76
The Spirit and the Bride	77
The Sorrows of Sin	82
Seeking a Lost Saviour	83
The Chiefest	84
The Altogether Lovely. — Gathered Lilies	85
She cometh as the Morning	91
Resting Unawares	92
Who is She that looketh forth as the Morning?	93
Lift me up, O Jesus	94
Going forth with Jesus	95
Leaning on the Arm of Jesus	96

OTHER POEMS.

	PAGE.
Holy Fear	101
Transforming Power of Prayer. — Talking of Calvary	102
Jesus Only	103
Good to be Here	104
Shut in	106
The Closet Hour	107
Away to the Mercy-Seat	108
Three Times a Day	109
Cast me not away from thy Presence. — Seeking Jesus	110
Waiting on the Lord	111
Cast thy Burden on the Lord	112
Peace	113
The Prisoner's Sigh	114
Love's Question	115
Trust in God	116
Words of Comfort. — Glory to the Nazarene	117
Morning Song	118
Evening Psalm	119
Longings. — Hymn of Consecration	121
Obedience	123
Our Father which art in Heaven	124
Be still, Poor Heart	125
Jesus, take me Home	126
Lost Joy	127
A Sweet Confession	128
Safety of the Good. — The Challenge of a Pure Heart	129
Perfect Peace	130
Secret Faults	131
The Lord's Secret	132
Pleasant Places	133
The Touch of Faith	134
The Fatal Delay	135
The Prodigal Son	136
Rest amidst Unrest	147
Soul Breathings	148
Rest, Rest! — If 'twern't for the Grace of God	149
Gethsemane	150
Thy Will, not Mine	153
The River of Life	154
Mary Magdalene	155
Sorrow and Joy	156

CONTENTS.

	PAGE.
Remember Me	157
The Wondrous on Before	158
The Desired Haven	159
Sabbath Eve	160
Even so, Come, Lord Jesus!	161
The Birthplace of a Soul. — The Power of Faith	162
The Young Ruler	163
The Guide and Goal	165
Stone Troubles	166
Waiting at the Pool	167
I passed down the Valley they say is so Lone	168
David's Cure for a Faint Heart	169
Consolation in Christ. — Light at Eventide	170
In the Strange Darkness. — Christ needs a Working Church	172
Incomprehensible Wealth	174
The Glorious Declaration	175
A Great Deep	176
Near God. — Waiting for the Angel	177
God knows	178
Man impeached by Nature	180
The Death of Time	187
U.S.A., 1873	188
Day	190
Night	191
Jesus of Nazareth passes by	193
The Ministry of Angels	194
Lightened by Looking	196
Language of Days	197
What of the Night?	198
And yet there is Room	199
What wilt thou do in the Swelling of Jordan?	200
Rare Knowledge. — The Testimony	201
Patient Waiting	202
Wrath of God and the Lamb	203
Immortality of the Soul	204

SOLOMON'S SONG RE-SUNG.

SOLOMON'S SONG RE-SUNG.

"THE SONG OF SONGS."

I.

To Christ the highest praise belongs
   In earth, or heaven above;
And he who sings this song of songs
   Must sing redeeming love.

Of nothing higher could we sing,
   Of nothing deeper dream;
And harps which heavenly anthems ring
   Have found no brighter theme.

He died for love of thee, my soul, —
   To hide thy guilty wrongs;
Now let thy sweetest numbers roll,
   And sing this song of songs.

II.

O Jesus, Jesus! spotless Lamb!
And didst thou die for me?
Now all I have, and all I am,
   I offer up to thee.

And didst thou wear the thorny crown
   To be my hope and trust?
Low at thy feet I now bow down,
   And worship in the dust.

And didst thou come from heaven above?
   The dead to life restore?
Oh, boundless depths and heights of love,
   Surround me evermore!

O Jesus, Jesus! to thy side
   For refuge now I flee,
And hide, O precious Saviour! hide
   All but thyself from me!

III.

O Cross of glory and of grace!
   Thou dost salvation give!
A loving, bleeding, dying face
   We see, and seeing, live.

O Cross of glory! let thy beams
   The fuller light impart;
O Blood of cleansing! let thy streams
   Now sanctify the heart.

O Cross of glory! while we sing,
   O'er all completely reign,
That we to thee may closer cling,
   And never sin again.

O Cross of glory and of grace!
   Thou dost salvation give;
And all our lost and ruined race
   May look to thee and live.

THE KISS OF JESUS.

"Let Him kiss me."

Kiss of Jesus is forgiving
   All the wrong the soul has wrought;
Leading it to holy living,
   Filling it with holy thought;
Changing all to snowy whiteness
   Sin had darkened with its stain,
Brightening with heavenly brightness
   Life, and making death a gain.

Kiss of Jesus is the blessing
   Of a Father's smiling face;
When the prodigal, confessing,
   Comes to ask the lowest place,
Feels the kiss of lips forgiving,
   Wounding only with a smile,
Though he had spent all his living
   With the vilest of the vile.

THE LOVE OF JESUS.

"Thy love is better than wine."

Wine a moment cheers the sad:
Love of Jesus maketh glad
All the life, and still doth fold
Spirit round when lips are cold.

Sunlight which can never fade,
Shelter which no storms invade,
Healing for each wounded breast,
Haven where the weary rest.

Love of Jesus, love divine,
Better far than choicest wine:
Light and life it doth impart
To the worn and weary heart.

Brightest when the clouds appear;
Nearest when the storms are near;
Sweetest when the cross we take,
Leaving all for Jesus' sake.

Nothing shall its brightness dim,
If we love and follow him,
Who, to bless us with his love,
Died, and intercedes above.

THE NAME OF JESUS.

"Thy name is as ointment poured forth."

I.

Thy name, O Lord! doth lustre shed,
As ointment poured upon the head;
And he who feels its saving grace
Will wear the glory in his face.

As ointment gives to death life-bloom,
Thy name prepares us for the tomb;
And by its power we shall arise
When thunders shake the earth and skies.

As ointment health to wound unseals,
Thy name a world of sorrow heals;
And wounds which baffled skill and fame
Heal at the mention of thy name.

Oh! help us each who know its worth,
To pour thy love as ointment forth,
And to a wounded world proclaim
The healing virtue of thy name.

II.

Jesus, thy name is all our trust,
    We have no hope beside.
Through thee at last our mouldering dust
    Will all be glorified.
Oh! teach us now by faith to claim
Each promise through thy mighty name.

We seek no love, dear Lord, but thine;
   We can no higher rise;
And where thy beams of mercy shine,
   Alone is paradise.
Oh may we now and ever see
That paradise regained by thee!

There is no solid joy below,
   Where death and sorrow meet;
There is no place of rest, we know,
   But sitting at thy feet.
Oh! give us all that blessed rest,
First at thy feet, then on thy breast.

MAN CONDEMNED BY ANGELS.

"The virgins love Thee."

If love from angels Christ doth win,
   How must their love condemn?
He only died for human sin,
   He never died for them.

They stand before his wounds and gaze;
   They talk of Calvary's hill,
And fill eternity with praise,
   While all the world is still.

They see the scars of nail and spear,
   Which tell of sorrow's weight;
And love him with a love more dear,
   While man alone doth hate.

They talk of Christ with holy pride —
    How he was lowly born;
While man, for whom he lived and died,
    Doth mention him with scorn.

When to the judgment nations go,
    And we appear with them,
The love for Jesus angels show
    Will all the world condemn.

HASTING TO FIND JESUS.

"We will run after Thee."

JUDGMENT-DAY, with storm and blast,
On before its shadows cast;
Earth no shelter doth provide,
Where the guilty soul may hide.
Jesus gives a refuge sweet:
We are hasting to his feet.

In his presence there is peace,
At his bidding sorrows cease:
Stain of sin and shade of fear
Vanish when his wounds sppear.
With our garments crimson dyed,
We are hasting to his side.

When he called, we gave no heed,
Answered not, nor felt our need;
Now all helpless, lost, undone,
After Jesus swift we run:
Weary, shelterless, and cold,
We are hasting to his fold.

Come! escape eternal loss;
Run with us to reach the cross;
Guilty soul, no more delay:
Shadows of the judgment-day
Fall around us! swiftly fly
To the cross while it is nigh.

GUESTS OF THE KING.

"The King hath brought me into his chambers."

How sweet to be the guest
   Of Jesus and his bride!
They brought me from the world to rest
   In chambers cool and wide.

Here in this cool retreat,
   Perfumed by praise and prayer,
I sit before the Master's feet,
   And learn his wisdom there.

This is the secret place,
   Where all the holy dwell,
Who fullest drink of saving grace,
   And love the Saviour well.

They have forsaken all
  The world and sinful lust:
They answered to the Saviour's call,
  And trust with perfect trust.

No shade of fear or doubt
  Can cross the sacred rooms;
And all the garden round about
  With hope and comfort blooms.

Here all who will may come;
  They call it perfect rest:
The Saviour hath prepared the home,
  And faith prepares the guest.

REJOICING IN JESUS.

"We will be glad and rejoice in Thee."

Awake, my soul! why art thou sad?
Rejoice in Jesus, and be glad:
Though worlds may roll in fire above,
He will surround thee with his love.

Rejoice in Jesus! he is strong
To shield the right, and crush the wrong;
His love for thee hath bound nor end:
In life, in death, he is thy Friend.

Rejoice in Jesus! by his pain
Thou shalt the life eternal gain;
For thee he suffered, heart and limb:
Rejoice, my soul! rejoice in him.

Lay all thy mourning robes aside;
For thee the Saviour lived and died;
And when he comes to earth again,
Thou shalt with him rejoice and reign.

REMEMBERING JESUS.

"We will remember Thy love."

I.

What heart in human bosom set,
The love of Jesus can forget?
Who, that has heard for whom he died,
Forgotten, lays that love aside?

O Jesus! in this sacred hour,
We celebrate thy saving power;
Remember now, with grateful hearts,
The comfort sweet thy love imparts.

No spot on earth is half so blest
As that where love of thine gave rest;
And we beheld with tearful eyes
A pathway open to the skies.

It was thy love which freedom gave,
When earthly power could shield nor save;
It is thy love which lights the gloom
Around the portals of the tomb.

Remembering thy love, we bow
Before thy feet, and bless thee now;
And till thy face in light we see,
With love we shall remember thee.

II.

Loving him whose blood was shed,
Take we now the wine and bread;
With the hallowed cross in view,
Vows of purity renew:
Thou from sin didst set us free;
Lord, we do remember thee.

We remember now the day
When our sins were washed away;
See the wounded side which blest
Heart and soul with perfect rest.
Lord, and can it ever be,
We should cease to think of thee?

While we take the bread and wine,
Fill our hearts with light divine;
Tasting emblems of thy love,
Raise our thoughts to heaven above:
Till thy face in bliss we see,
May we still remember thee!

III.

Who can describe the bitter cup,
    Filled with our nature's dross?
All language fails when we take up
    The story of the cross.

As we think o'er the painful years
   Endured by our dear Lord,
We tell the story with our tears,
   But cannot speak a word.

Remembering thy toil and pain,
   Dear Saviour, we would not
Re-open thy deep wounds again
   By sinful word or thought.

If we deny the Saviour's name,
   His hallowed cross disown,
We put him to an open shame
   Before his Father's throne.

But let us prove by word and deed,
   We choose that better part;
Nor cause the Saviour's side to bleed,
   Nor wound the Saviour's heart.

THE LORD OUR RIGHTEOUSNESS.

"I am black, but comely."

NOUGHT of merit we possess,
Jesus is our righteousness:
Moons with borrowed glory roll,
So through Jesus shines the soul.
Black we are when wandering wide,
We are comely at his side.

All the righteousness we own
Came from Christ, and him alone;
He hath robed us in the dress
Of his own pure righteousness.
Though so black, beneath its light
We are comely in his sight.

BEARING REPROACH FOR JESUS.

"My mother's children were angry with me."

Though brother, sister, friends, forsake,
The cross of Jesus I will take;
Though kindred hearts with anger burn,
I dare not from the Saviour turn.

I well can bear the scorn a while
If Jesus cheers me with his smile;
Undaunted meet a frowning host,
And pray for those who scorn the most.

Alone the cross my Saviour bore,
Alone the thorny crown he wore;
The world oppressed, disciples fled,
And strangers begged his body, dead.

I follow where my Saviour trod,
Though scorned of men, beloved of God:
On earth I share with him the frown,
Hereafter wear with him the crown.

DENYING SELF FOR OTHERS.

"They made me keeper of the vineyards; but mine own vineyard have I not kept."

My soul has soared to heaven above,
    And caught its breathings glad,
For others sung of hope and love,
    When heart of mine was sad.

I've tended vineyards all around,
    While they who owned them slept;
And in the end have sadly found
    My vineyard was not kept.

But loving man is loving God,
    And loving self is sin:
The heart that sheds its love abroad
    More blessing gathers in.

Denying self for others' weal
    Is bearing Jesus' cross;
To live, and not for others feel,
    Is an eternal loss.

THE PASTOR.

"They made me keeper of the vineyards."

This vineyard God hath given,
    And great the weight I bear,
To guard the ripened fruit for heaven,
    And tend the vines with care.

Here to the Living Vine
    We graft the old and young;
And infant tendrils gently twine
    Where ripened fruits are hung.

The Living Vine its shade
    Doth o'er the vineyard cast,
That bud and blossom may not fade
    Beneath the storm and blast.

It life to all supplies,
    And never can exhaust:
No branch for lack of nurture dies,
    Nor vine is ever lost.

I cannot toil alone,
    Nor give to all my care:
The church must make the work its own,
    And each a burden bear.

Then Christ will say, "Well done!"
    His blessing sweet impart,
If every great and lowly one
    Will nobly do his part.

THE PASTOR'S CONFESSION.

"Mine own vineyard have I not kept."

Thy fruitful life, O Lord, impart,
For barren, barren, is my heart:
Before thy cross I sadly mourn,
Too little fruit my life has borne.

The ceaseless toil, the weight of care,
Has wounded faith and weakened prayer:
That others ripened fruit might gain,
My vineyard has neglected lain.

Reveal, O Lord! thy boundless love,
Send light and cleansing from above;
And draw me near the mercy-seat,
To lay my burdens at thy feet.

Forgive the past, the future bless,
Thy servant's vineyard newly dress;
That to thy glory and thy praise
Rich fruit may crown the coming days.

WHERE FEEDEST THOU?

"Tell me, O thou whom my soul loveth, where thou feedest."

Where feedest thou? with angels bright,
On shores of rest, by seas of light?
Where deathless blossoms shed perfume
O'er white robed guests and banquet room?

Oh tell me, in what court above
Thou feedest, whom my soul doth love!
That I may see thy table spread,
And gather crumbs of living bread.

With angels Jesus doth not feed;
But all the poor who feel their need,
And contrite hearts with sorrow crowned,
Are feasting at his table found.

The outcast, sinful, crimson dyed
Doth Jesus welcome to his side;
With all who trust, of every creed,
The Saviour comes, unseen, to feed.

To every contrite heart he brings
A pleasant feast of heavenly things;
And all on earth who taste his love
Shall feast with him in heaven above.

THE NOONTIDE REST.

"Thou makest thy flock to rest at noon."

I.

Amidst the noon of toil and care,
    The Lord a rest provides,
Where all the flocks together share
    Its cooling shades and tides.

When heat of conflict fiercest burns,
    The church is sore opprest,
Then Christ the tide of battle turns,
    And gives his people rest.

The toiler seeks at noon the shade,
    Secure from scorching sun:
So hath the cross a shadow made
    For every weary one.

O weary ones! in noontide heat,
　　Borne down by grief and care,
Turn to the Saviour's rest so sweet,—
　　Refresh yourselves with prayer.

II.

Rest is found in sitting lowly
　　At the feet of wounded love;
Learning to be pure and holy,
　　As the sainted hosts above.

Laying down the things that please us,
　　Dogmas, form, and classic scrolls,
Taking up the yoke of Jesus
　　Brings sweet rest unto our souls.

Rest is found in the forgiving
　　Wrongs, a bosom friend has wrought;
And through all our future, living
　　Just as though he'd wronged us not.

Every morning, heart engages
　　For a glad or tearful way;
Each to-morrow brings the wages
　　For the deeds of yesterday.

Hearts indulge in light behavior,
　　Cherish thoughts that please them best,
Then, at evening, ask the Saviour
　　For the blessed gift of rest;

Wonder why they don't obtain it,
   Blame the preacher, church, and hell,
When the only way to gain it
   Is to serve the Saviour well.

III.

Watchmen, are you growing weary,
   Watching night and watching day?
Do the hours seem long and dreary,
   Till the shadows clear away?
Grasp the standard, hold it tighter,
   Meet the foe midst shot and shell;
Heavenly rest will be the lighter
   If you do your duty well.

Burdened hearts, by sorrow shaken,
   Left alone in tears to grieve,
By the friends of youth forsaken,
   Whom you dreamed would never leave;
Let your hopes be centred only
   On the Saviour's changeless love;
There's a rest for all the lonely
   In the heavenly home above.

Christian, are thy crosses growing
   Heavier, and the journey long?
Art thou saddened with the knowing
   Right is conquered by the wrong?
Strive a little longer, bearing
   All, though drooping spirits mourn;
Crowns will be more worth the wearing
   If the cross is nobly borne.

Brothers, sisters, toiling, praying,
    Seeking for the higher rest,
Oh the joy of weary, laying
    Ever on the Saviour's breast;
Where the parted friends are meeting,
    Never more to parted be,
Where the angels shout their greeting
    All across the crystal sea.

Here is but the time of testing,
    Time of battle, tears, and pain:
There the joy of sweetly resting,
    Never more to toil again.
Let us, then, bear all the sorrow
    God shall deem it wise and best;
Soon will dawn the glorious morrow,
    With its sweet, eternal rest.

DARKNESS.

"Why should I be as one that turneth aside by the flocks of thy companions?"

THE Christian, with affliction tried,
May seem as one that turns aside
From duty's path, — may see the dawn
Of God's approving smile withdrawn.

Amidst the flocks, by Jesus led,
He hungers, while the rest are fed;
And seeing joys to him denied,
He feels as one that turns aside.

Such times of darkness have opprest
The hearts that love the Saviour best;
And midst the shadows rudely tossed,
They dreamed that heaven and all were lost.

Why shouldst thou seem as one that turns,
While love for Jesus in thee burns?
Why, with companions thou hast known,
Dost feel a stranger and alone?

The shadows on thy spirit thrust
Are only sent to try thy trust;
And Christ reveals the morning light
To all who follow through the night.

FORSAKING JESUS.

"One that turneth aside."

To leave the Saviour's wounded side
   Is leaving all that's best;
On seas of anguish drifting wide
   From everlasting rest.

Can trump of fame make pure the heart?
   Can gold supply the loss?
Or homage of a world impart
   The comfort of the cross?

He loses rest who looks behind;
   He loses life who turns
From the Redeemer of mankind,
   And all his mercy spurns.

Forsake temptations round thee thrown,
  From every bondage break;
Forsake the dearest idol known,
  But never Christ forsake.

FOLLOW THE GOOD.

"Go thy way by the footsteps of the flock."

Follow sect, nor follow creed,
Lean upon no broken reed
Human wisdom brings to lure
Heart from following the pure.

Ages cannot hide from view
Footsteps of the good and true;
Safe through martyr fires they trod,
Finding rest while serving God.

Follow men, who midst the flame
Sung a world-redeeming name;
Stood the test of fire and sword,
Rather than betray their Lord.

Follow men, who for the cross
Suffered every earthly loss,—
Living, dying, sung the theme,
Jesus! mighty to redeem!

Follow, follow where they lead;
Jesus doth such heroes need,
That his banner, crimson-dyed,
May be carried far and wide.

THE CHILDREN FOR JESUS.

"Feed thy kids by the shepherds' tents."

The children for Jesus! Oh! carry them in
To his tents, that shepherds may shield them from
    sin;
Let them feed with the pure, the true, and the good,
On a gospel of life, the heavenly food.

The children for Jesus! he waits to impart
The wisdom which cleanses, to each youthful
    heart;
On earth he embraced them, and waits now above,
To welcome them all to the banquet of love.

The children for Jesus! each little one bring,
Of Jesus to learn and of Jesus to sing;
The Lord did not die for the learned and few, —
He died for the great, and the little ones too.

The children for Jesus! Oh! gather them in,
For under the cross they are shielded from sin:
If none are too young to pass over death's tide,
Then none are too young to know Jesus has died.

FUTURE TRIUMPH.

"We will make thee borders of gold with studs of silver."

The Saviour will hereafter crown
  What he in us has wrought;
And on our spirits shower down
  Rich blessings, passing thought.

We taste his mercy here in part;
  But near his throne above,
He will bestow on every heart
  Eternal weight of love.

The gold and silver of his grace
  Will on our garments gleam,
When we behold the loving face
  Which sorrowed to redeem.

Here ample feasts the Spirit serves,
  Of mercy and of love;
Yet gold and silver he reserves
  For banquet-rooms above.

STRENGTH AND BEAUTY OF THE CHURCH.

"I have compared thee, O my love! to a company of horses in Pharaoh's chariots."

Press onward, Church of God most high!
Thy chariot wheels should swifter fly!
Thy strength and beauty God has given
To win and take the world for heaven.

Sweep through the land, its breadth and length!
The Lord of Hosts shall be thy strength!
Thrill all the world with strains of peace,
Till every sound of discord cease.

With love's own beauty thou canst win
Each wayward heart, forgiving sin ;
In Jesus' strength go forth, and free
This world, for that which is to be.

Fly, chariot, fly! and bear afar
A holy band for holy war ;
Thy messages of peace proclaim,
Till all rejoice in Jesus' name.

LOVE'S OFFERING.

"While the king sitteth at his table, my spikenard sendeth forth the smell thereof."

Bowed at the feet of Jesus, low,
My humble praises sweetly flow ;
He smells the odor all the while,
And deigns to bless me with a smile.

Beneath the sunbeams and the showers,
All fragrant grow the gentle flowers :
So 'neath the smile of Jesus' face,
Doth fragrant grow each bloom of grace.

And Christian hearts in praise and prayer
Give back what Christ hath planted there ;
The more they give, the more they fill,
And giving all are fragrant still.

The odor of the grateful heart
A joy to Jesus doth impart ;
And more acceptable shall rise
Than fragrant gales from paradise.

THE PRECIOUSNESS OF JESUS.

"A bundle of myrrh is my well-beloved unto me."

What strength of love, what healing balm,
    The name of Jesus bears;
Surrounding heart and soul with calm,
    Amidst a world of cares.

When thoughts of sin break our repose,
    And tears of sorrow fall,
The blood of Jesus gently flows,
    And sweetly whitens all.

How precious in affliction's hour,
    To know the Saviour chose
The weight of pain's oppressing power,
    That he might heal our woes.

How precious to the wounded breast,
    Which from the tempter flies,
To find that peaceful, sheltered rest
    The love of Christ supplies.

How precious, every step we take,
    O'er life's uneven way,
To know that Jesus, for our sake,
    In heaven doth ever pray.

How precious, when at death's cold tide,
    We sink, with fear oppressed,
To find the Saviour at our side,
    And pass with him to rest.

FAITHFULNESS.

"He shall lie all night betwixt my breasts."

When shadows fall, and sunbeams flee,
O Jesus! still abide with me;
Depart not with departing day,—
I need thee most when dark the way.

Though lost to sight, I shall rejoice
To hear the music of thy voice;
And safely reach the morning land,
If through the dark thou hold my hand.

Abide, O Saviour! be my guest,
With thee alone my heart can rest:
I feel, in darkest hour, no fear,
And welcome death, if thou art near.

O Saviour! dark though it may be,
With simple trust I cling to thee;
For soon I know upon my sight
Will sweetly dawn the morning light.

THE GREAT RESTORATIVE.

"My beloved is unto me as a cluster of camphire in the vineyards of En-gedi."

The Saviour doth restore,
  By merits of his death,
A ruined world which sank before
  Decay's devouring breath.

The camphire cluster springs
   Amidst the dreary tomb;
And all the dead and mouldering things
   Burst into bud and bloom.

Lost glory comes again,
   New life inspires the dead;
And barren hearts with beauty reign,
   From clustered virtues shed.

The odor of the cross
   A drooping world revives;
And changes into gold the dross
   Of all our sinful lives.

CHANGED.

"Behold, thou art fair, my love! thou hast doves' eyes."

I once was all defiled,
   Nor dared to look above,
Till Jesus on my spirit smiled,
   And filled me with his love.

Now purified I am,
   And sinless walk each day;
All glory, glory to the Lamb!
   Which bore my sins away.

My soul so black has been,
   But Jesus calls me fair:
His precious blood hath washed me clean,
   His righteousness I wear.

Mine eyes once fierce with sin,
  Are changed like the doves';
A holy quiet reigns within,
  And Christ the Love of loves.

THE CHURCH IN THE WORLD.

"As the lily among thorns, so is my love among the daughters."

The Church her holy light doth shed
  On all the world around;
And pilgrim feet, that heavenward tread,
  Within her courts are found.

She walks by dark and thorny ways,
  And often wounded, bleeds;
But still she works, and still she prays,
  Nor faints, while Jesus leads.

She falters not when wounded sore,
  But walks with firmer tread:
A crown of thorns her master wore
  When he for sinners bled.

Though institutions loudly call
  For aid, till mines exhaust,
Her mission is above them all, —
  She seeks to save the lost.

And he that talent, time, or store,
  Upon her altar lays,
Doth give a blessing evermore
  To all the human race.

THE HOUSE OF GOD.

"The beams of our house are cedar, and our rafters of fir."

That God whom heaven cannot contain
Delights in earthly courts to reign;
In temples built by human hand
He dwells, the God of every land.

And where the holy meet to pray,
He doth his saving power display;
Beneath the cedar and the fir
He meets his church and blesses her.

Not shifting tents, on desert lone,
But an abiding house we own;
Where, every day through all the seven,
The manna falls to us from heaven.

And while his presence here we share,
The Lord of Hosts, he doth prepare
A house, not made with hands, above,
For all who seek and share his love.

THE LOVELINESS OF JESUS.

"I am the Rose of Sharon."

How lovely did thy leaves unfold,
 Thou heavenly-moulded flower!
And in thy nature we behold
 All beauty and all power.

When in the stall thou didst repose,
    And wise men round thee came,
They looked on Sharon's beauteous rose,
    And knew thy ancient name.

Reared in a lowly cottage room,
    And early taught to toil,
Doth tell how fairest flowers may bloom
    Upon the rudest soil.

The fragrance of a life so pure,
    The memory of each deed,
Shall through eternity endure,
    And heaven with wonder feed.

For when the Roman spear and nail
    Did beat upon its bloom,
For all mankind there did exhale
    An ever sweet perfume.

CHRIST PRE-EMINENT.

"As the apple among the trees of the wood, so is my beloved among the sons."

Pre-eminent is Christ o'er all,
    In earth, or heaven above;
The angels into nothing fall,
    O'ershadowed by his love.

Ten thousand worlds, with glory bright,
    Before his presence dim;
And heaven itself, with all her light,
    Is swallowed up in him.

The mystery of God and man
  In one, to suffering brought,
Revealed, doth still withhold a plan
  That baffles power of thought.

The angels sing, and ever sing
  About the wounds he bore;
While every look new wonders bring
  They never sung before.

No throne is higher than his throne;
  Before him nothing was;
While all created things make known
  His handiwork and laws.

The purest spirits Christ adore,
  The highest kiss his feet;
And age to age, for evermore,
  His praises shall repeat.

UNDER THE CROSS.

"I sat down under his shadow with great delight."

Under the cross I now sit with delight;
Jesus, my Saviour, hath clothed me in white;
I see the blood flow all day from his side,
And keep ever near the sin-cleansing tide.

Under the cross there's a shadow so sweet,
That shields from the blast and hides from the heat:
There never comes pain and never comes loss,
Under the shadow of Jesus's cross.

Under the cross, all the purest and best
Come for the shadow and substance of rest;
And they who the name of Jesus denied,
May come to the cross — its shadow will hide.

All who on seas of temptation now toss,
Come to the shadow of Jesus's cross;
Ye who have lingered till late in life's day,
Come to the shadow, no longer delay.

Come old and come young, come feeble, come all,
To the cross, while yet its shadow doth fall;
It shields now in time, and shields in that day
When heaven and earth are passing away.

HOLY LIVING.

"His fruit was sweet to my taste."

The fruit of loving deeds,
    The fruit of holy thought,
For lasting sweetness far exceeds
    The fruit by pleasure brought.

To live for Christ alone,
    And serve him every day,
Will bring us fruit to ripeness grown,
    When time has passed away.

The fruit of Jesus' love
    Is ours to possess;
On earth below, in heaven above,
    It evermore will bless.

No angel can declare
　　The fruit of Calvary's tree;
It still will boundless blessings bear
　　Through all eternity.

HOME AT LAST.

"He brought me to his banqueting house."

I.

Home, sweet home! I'm there at last,
Love of Christ around me cast;
From the cross I long did roam,
Jesus brought me safely home.
Home, and all the danger past,
Home in Jesus' love at last!

Oh how blest the new-found rest,
Leaning on the Saviour's breast!
Oh what wonders, passing thought,
Jesus' cleansing blood hath wrought!
Home at last! at Jesus' side
Evermore will I abide.

Oh how kind must Jesus be
To have sought so long for me,
And prepare so rich a feast
For the heart that loved him least!
All I know of love so vast
Is that I am home at last!

II.

I heard a voice from Calvary's holy mountain,
    Speaking in accents tender to my soul:
It bade me come and wash in that pure fountain,
    Whose waters heal and make forever whole.

I was afar off, then, amid the singing
    And the fierce sunshine of earth's gilded dross;
But when I heard that voice so sweetly ringing,
    I turned and sought the shadow of the cross.

Zionward it lay, o'erarched with glory,
    Set in the breast of earth, but pointing up;
Telling, with language sweet, the wondrous story
    Of him, who, thorn-crowned, drank the bitter cup.

I thought of all my meanness, and was turning
    To earth again, and all her gilded dross:
But oh! that voice came full of deepest yearning,
    And wooed me to the shadow of the cross.

LOVE'S BANNER.

"His banner over me was love."

Love is the banner which over us waves,
Jesus, our Captain, who blesses and saves;
We march all the day, his banner in sight,
Round us it folds when we slumber at night.

On Calvary's hill it first was unfurled,
Dyed crimson with blood that ransoms a world;
And he who now bears it, bled but to win
Souls from the thraldom of sorrow and sin.

Follow that banner of refuge and love,
Who seek for a home with Jesus above.
The sinful and lost its blessings may share,
And all who a cross for Jesus will bear.

To day it is love; it may bring us pain
When earthward it sweeps with Jesus again:
Its welcomes so sweet may never more wave,
O follow it now, and Jesus will save.

OVER-JOY.*

"Stay me with flagons, comfort me with apples, for I am sick of love."

i.

What feasts of rapture and delight
  With Christ, my Lord, I share!
And scenes that burst upon my sight
  Are more than clay can bear.

He tells the story of his love,
  In undertones so sweet,
Till heaven sinks round me from above
  While sitting at his feet.

---

*In the last sickness of J. Welch, he was overheard saying, "Lord, hold thine hand, it is enough; thy servant is a clay vessel, and can hold no more."

I know my sins did wound him sore,
    And rest of mine destroy;
But still he loves me more and more,
    And breaks my heart with joy.

A moment, Lord, thy wounds conceal,
    A moment light deny;
For if thou dost more love reveal,
    My soul with joy will die.

II.

Oh the joy of early seeking,
    Early finding Jesus out,
And to hear him sweetly speaking
    Into silence every doubt.

Daily rising higher, higher,
    Toward the sunlight and the dawn;
All the weight of base desire,
    All the power of passion, gone.

Soul expanding, thought refining,
    Breaking fetters, winging way
Upward, to the cloudless shining
    Of the everlasting day.

Feeling God is growing dearer,
    Watches you with tender care;
Feeling heaven is growing nearer
    Every time you kneel in prayer.

Old delights and sinful pleasures
  Falling backward, beaten, dead:
Yearnings after heavenly treasures
  Fill the heart, the soul, the head.

This is joy, the rest of leaning
  On that cross which points above;
Drinking in the hidden meaning
  Of the Saviour's boundless love.

O thou King of Glory! enter
  This poor heart and triumph, till
Every wandering thought shall centre
  In obedience to thy will.

DIVINE SUPPORT AND PROTECTION.

"His left hand is under my head, and his right hand doth embrace me."

Sweet is thy rest my heart,
  Secure thy hiding place;
The tempter's power shall never part
  Thee from thy Lord's embrace.

His left hand doth sustain,
  His right hand sweetly soothe;
While hidden things but grow more plain,
  And heavenward paths more smooth.

What foe hast thou to fear?
  What thing can bring thee harm,
While God himself is ever near
  To shield thee with his arm?

Repose in perfect trust,
　　Though all the world assail;
The throne of God must fall to dust
　　Before thy faith can fail.

II.

We all can trust God when the light
　　Of health gilds us and ours;
But can we do it when the blight
　　Falls on love's cherished flowers?

'Tis well to say, " Thy will be done!"
　　When bright days on us crowd;
But can we do it when the sun
　　Sinks down behind a cloud?

Our God is wise, we whisper now,
　　The prospect seems so fair;
But can we say it when the brow
　　Is furrowed o'er by care?

There is no light without its shade,
　　No day without its night;
And we are not as angels, made
　　To dwell in cloudless light.

God needs must pass us through the fire,
　　We are so full of dross;
And when he wills to raise us higher,
　　He makes us bear the cross.

Though death should set from us apart
　　Love's most beloved face,
The language of the broken heart
　　Should be a song of praise.

BEHOLD, HE COMETH!

"The voice of my beloved! behold, he cometh, leaping upon the mountains and skipping upon the hills."

I.

The Saviour comes! I hear his cry,
It shakes the earth and rends the sky;
The mountains melt beneath his tread,
And graves restore their borrowed dead.

Oh what a day! the thunders crash,
The cities fall, the lightnings flash!
O'er skies so blue an hour ago
A sea of fire beats to and fro.

The stars are falling: moon and sun
In flames are flying: time is done!
And they who Jesus' name denied
Are calling on the rocks to hide.

He comes! he comes! the Lamb once slain
With glory comes to earth again:
The saints, rejoicing, hail their king,
And swell the song his angels sing.

II.

Behold, I come quickly! Christ comes not again
In garments of flesh, as a lamb to be slain:
He came with a cross, but he comes with a crown,
And the thrones of this world shall all be cast down.

BEHOLD, HE COMETH!

Hail, Jesus, we hail thee! the bright morning
    star,
That leads us to glory from darkness afar;
Thy light, the great prophets saw, circling their
    dreams;
That light now is o'er us, we bask in its beams.

Behold, I come quickly! O Christian, work on!
The night is fast waning, full soon comes the
    dawn:
"Well done! good and faithful," thy Master will
    say,
When he makes up his jewels in the soul-trying
    day.

For the cross thou hast borne so patient and
    long,
He will give thee a crown, a harp, and a song;
And with the redeemed ones from nations un-
    known,
Thy praise shall ascend to the Lamb and his
    throne.

Behold, I come quickly! the Saviour has said,
Whose word is a life-throb which cannot grow
    dead.
The world cried "away!" in his sorrowing hour;
But who shall upbraid when he comes in his
    power?

No thorns on his brow, and no wound in his side,
To tell how he suffered, or tell how he died;
But circled by angels that sing a new hymn,
And the light of a day that cannot grow dim.

SORROW PAST.

"Lo, the winter is past, the rain is over and gone."

Gone is now the winter dreary,
    Which has been with us so long,
Making heart and spirit weary,
    Waiting for the summer song.

Overhead the clouds are breaking,
    And the last fall of the rain
Now in arch of light is making
    Promise not to come again.

So the clouds of pain and sadness
    Leave us but to sing their loss;
While the dawn of rest and gladness
    Breaks upon us from the cross.

Clouds of doubt are breaking o'er us;
    Winter from the soul has fled;
And with joy we see before us
    Fount of blood for sinners shed.

FOLLOWING JESUS.

"Rise up, my love, my fair one, and come away."

Farewell to the world, attractive and gay;
Since Jesus has called, I will not delay;
The pleasures of wealth my heart shall resign,
Nor mourn o'er their loss, for Jesus is mine.

I heard his voice call, arise, come away!
While sinful companions pressed me to stay;
But friends cannot hold, nor pleasure beguile,
Since Jesus has given the light of his smile.

My will I resign, and count it no loss,
Each duty perform, and carry my cross;
No danger I fear, nor wearied can be,
For Jesus in heaven is waiting for me.

O hold me not back! I seek for the prize
Of life that's eternal, there in the skies;
A gleam of its light already I see,
And Jesus in heaven is calling for me.

The follies of youth, I lay them aside,
With passions that burn: lust, anger, and pride;
From all that is sin I ever am free,
For Jesus in heaven is praying for me.

TOKENS OF LOVE.

"The flowers appear on the earth."

ALL over the land there are tokens of love,
The promise of fruit for the Master above;
The winter is past, the summer is near,
And blossoms of hope in the churches appear.

The hearts that so long richest mercy denied
Are asking for Jesus, and seeking his side;
The feeble and doubting now break from their fear,
The harvest is coming, and summer is near.

Now faith looks above with a glory-lit eye,
While prayer spreads her wings, and she soars
   to the sky;
The promises shine out more lovely and clear,
For harvest is coming, and summer is near.

Blow wind from the east, and blow wind from the
   west;
Come, Spirit of God, let the people not rest;
Give birth to the sigh and the penitent tear,
Which tell us that summer and harvest are near.

A TIME OF JOY.

"The time of the singing of birds is come."

I.

THE summer has come with its blossom and song;
The churches awake that have slumbered so long.
Full harvests spread white on the far-stretching
   plain,
And reapers for Jesus, they gather the grain.

The seed of the kingdom through dark, weary
   years,
Half doubting its power, we scattered in tears;
But rooted, it grew through the long winter rain,
And reapers for Jesus, they gather the grain.

Weak faith now rejoices, beholding the sheaves,
And hope, more triumphant, her melody weaves:
We sing, and the angels re-echo the strain,
While reapers for Jesus, they gather the grain.

Now gone is the winter, its doubting and fear,
While two worlds rejoice that the harvest is here:
A time of refreshing is with us again,
And reapers for Jesus, they gather the grain.

II.

The windows of heaven are opening to-day,
And rich showers of blessing drop down on our way;
Too long we've been faithless, and doubting the Lord
Was willing to bless by fulfilling his word.

The heart of the sinner, though hardened so long,
Is melted, finds peace, and rejoices in song;
While they who in weakness the journey have trod,
Are strengthened within by the Spirit of God.

All praise to the Lamb for the blood that redeems,
The fountain for cleansing, and mercy's free streams;
All praise to the Spirit, whose quickening power
Has led us to seek and to welcome the shower.

Our vineyard rejoices, the vine-dresser sees
Rich fruit ripen fast on the once barren trees;
And they that bore well, until sapless they grew,
Begin now to put forth their blossoms anew.

SABBATH SCHOOL REVIVAL.

"The fig-tree putteth forth her green figs, and the vines with the tender grapes give a good smell."

Tender grapes on vines appear,
Christ among the children dear
Now is working by his grace,
Leading them to seek his face.
Love's own banner o'er us waves,
Christ the little children saves.

Finding Christ in early years
Saves from sorrow, pain, and tears;
Serving him from youth to age
Maketh life a stainless page:
Come, dear children, meekly bow
At the feet of Jesus now.

Parents for you ever pray,
Lest your little feet should stray
From the path by Jesus trod,
Which alone leads up to God.
Come with us, and praying, bow,
Give your hearts to Jesus now.

LITTLE SINS.

"Take us, the little foxes, that spoil the vines."

Where the river broad begins,
   But a streamlet flows:
So the force of little sins
   Widens as it goes.

Little insects pierce the ships
    Till a wreck they lie:
Little sins of heart and lips
    Ruin you and I.

Little foxes spoil the vine
    Tearing limbs apart:
Little sins will undermine
    Walls built round the heart.

Little sins forge strongest chains
    For the erring soul;
Little sins leave deepest stains
    On the judgment scroll.

IN THE ROCK I'M HIDING.

"Thou art in the clefts of the rock."

I.

Happy they who enter
To love's blissful centre;
Evermore beholding
Depths of grace unfolding.
    All to Christ confiding,
    Safe from sin abiding,
    In the Rock I'm hiding,
        Rock once cleft for me.

Gone the sorrow wearing,
Gone the burden bearing;
Christ hath undertaken
Weight of sins forsaken.
    All to Christ, etc.

Here the blood is flowing,
Purest life bestowing;
And no foe molesting,
Heart in Jesus resting.
        All to Christ, etc.

All by faith may enter
To love's blissful centre;
Where the blood of Jesus
From all bondage frees us.
        All to Christ, etc.

II.

Oh how sweet it is to hide
In the Saviour's wounded side;
Where each moment blood doth flow
Washing whiter than the snow,
Changing all my worn attire
Into seraph robes of fire.

How wast wrought my hiding place;
There is on thee still the trace
Of the Roman spear, whose thrust
Gave the wound in which I trust,—
Wound to which my soul has fled,
Till the judgment wake the dead.

Never more shall form or face
Lure me from my hiding place;
Base desire or poisoned dart
Cannot reach my shielded heart;
Nor the demon doubt molest,
In this riven side of rest.

THE DESIRE OF JESUS.

"Let me see thy countenance, let me hear thy voice; for sweet is thy voice, and thy countenance is comely."

The voice of the sinner to Jesus is sweet,
When pleading for mercy he comes to his feet:
That face is the fairest which leaves the world's
 dross,
And turns to the sunshine of Christ and his cross.

No angel so fair to the Saviour appears
As sinners set free from the thraldom of years;
No music of heaven such sweetness can bear
As sighs from a soul with its first broken prayer.

No anthem of praise sheds such rapture above
As spirits once lost singing Jesus's love;
He views with delight what his wounded heart
 won;
The Father, well-pleased, sees the work of his
 Son.

MINE AND HIS.

"My beloved is mine, and I am his."

All the wealth in Christ I own,
Angel tongue could not make known;
Nor can aught in heaven above
Tell the riches of his love.
This I know, and only this:
He is mine, and I am his.

Mine to love, and loving, see
His undying love for me;
Mine to serve, and serving, grow
More like him who loves me so:
This the crowning song of bliss:
He is mine, and I am his.

He who Jesus doth possess
Hath all blessing that can bless;
Hath all joy, all life, all love,
Filling earth or heaven above.
All is swallowed up in this:
He is mine, and I am his.

Heaven nothing higher sings,
Knowledge nothing deeper brings;
What eternity reveals
Is the wealth this truth conceals;
Boundless heights and depths of bliss!
He is mine, and I am his.

CHRIST AND HIS LILIES.

"He feedeth among the lilies."

Christ alone delights to feed
With the pure in thought and deed;
Sweetly he reveals his face
To the lilies of his grace.
While their snow-white leaves outspread,
Catch the dews and sunshine shed.

Unobtrusive, quiet, blest,
'Neath the shade of wings they rest ;
From the busy world apart
Place they share in Jesus' heart :
While his cross, with shadow sweet,
Shields them from the cold and heat.

When they bloom their purest white,
Stainless as the morning light,
Christ doth gently bear above
All the lilies of his love,
And 'neath softer, fairer skies,
They re-bloom in Paradise.

WAITING FOR THE DAWN.

"Until the day break and the shadows flee away, turn,
my beloved."

I.

Waiting for the dawn !
　Jesus, on us smile !
Till the night is gone,
　Turn, oh turn a while !
Lest from duty's path we stray
Ere the shadows flee away.

We would reach thy feet
　In the morning light ;
Foes unseen we meet,
　Darker grows the night.
Lord, from thy divine abode,
Lighten all this darksome road.

Jesus, lead us on!
  Guide and counsel be,
Till the morning dawn,
  And the shadows flee;
That we safely find our way
To the light of endless day.

II.

This is the night before the morning.
  Stars are fading through the dawn,
  Moons are waning, midnight gone;
  Slowly up the eastern way
  Roll the chariot wheels of day;
  While the universe makes room
  For the tragic play of doom.

This is the night before the morning.
  Dead hearts into beating break,
  Dead eyes into brightness wake.
  Hands unclasp upon the breast,
  Millions rise from their long rest;
  Leaving grave and leaving tomb
  For the tragic play of doom.

This is the night before the morning.
  Sea spreads her wave-wings to fly,
  When the angel passes by;
  Earth unfolds her worn attire
  For a mystic change of fire;
  And amidst the parting gloom
  Waits the tragic play of doom.

This is the night before the morning.
    Through the gates of heaven doth ride
    Bridegroom forth to meet his bride ;
    She is coming, clothed in white,
    From the chambers of the night,
    Forth to meet him in the light.
    Angels crowd, with wreath and plume,
    To the tragic play of doom.

This is the night before the morning.
    Flash the stars, by tempests driven,
    Trailing fire from heaven to heaven ;
    Lightnings, from far distance hurled,
    With their flame lips kiss the world :
    And midst fire, wail, light, and gloom,
    Opes the tragic play of doom.

SEEKING REST IN SECLUSION.

*"By night on my bed I sought him whom my soul loveth;
I sought him, but found him not."*

To the still and deep seclusion,
    Far from friend and guest,
Guilty fears will force intrusion,
    Breaking all the rest.

Not to deepest shades retreating
    Can one joy impart,
While within us there is beating
    Unforgiven heart.

Though no voice or shadow longer
    O'er our pathway crossed,
Voice within would speak the stronger,
    Lost! forever lost!

Rest comes not to highest heaven,
    Nor on earth appears,
While the heart is unforgiven,
    Though we seek with tears.

FOUND.

"I found him whom my soul loveth."

In the Almighty's earthly dwelling,
    Worn and crushed by pain and loss,
I have listened to the telling
    Of the story of the cross.

There the watchman stood and pointed,
    Till my soul could plainly see
Dying Jesus, God's anointed,
    With an open side for me.

Long I trembled, doubting, viewing
    Thorny crown and bleeding limb;
Fearing, while for mercy suing,
    When I should but trust in him.

Nearer, ever nearer creeping,
    Drawn by love divine and sweet,
Till, amidst a flood of weeping,
    I fell down and kissed his feet.

Then there came a sweet forgiving,
  Blood that cleansed from sinful dross:
Then commenced that purer living,
  Which springs only from the cross.

SEEKING REST IN THE WORLD.

"I will rise now, and go about the city in the streets, and in the broadways. I will seek him whom my soul loveth: I sought him, but found him not."

Sorrowful and wounded breast,
In the world dost seek for rest?
Cleansing for one guilty spot?
Thou wilt seek, but find it not.

In the gay and giddy tide
Seekest thou from God to hide?
Place where guilt is all forgot?
Thou wilt seek, but find it not.

Thinkest thou that sweetest song
Charms to silence voice of wrong?
Or that pleasure hides one blot?
Thou wilt seek, but find it not.

Thinkest thou the world has wrought
Change of life and change of thought?
Sin one lasting joy begot?
Thou wilt seek, but find it not.

THE COMING OF LOVE.

"Who is this that cometh out of the wilderness like pillars of smoke, perfumed with myrrh and frankincense, with all powders of the merchant?"

I.

Morn of glory breaks around us,
    Jesus comes, Jesus comes!
Fetters fall that long have bound us,
    Jesus comes, Jesus comes!
  Hallelujah, see the glory!
  Hallelujah, tell the story!
Hallelujah, hallelujah, Jesus comes!

See the tear of sorrow falling,
    Jesus comes, Jesus comes!
Hear the lost for mercy calling,
    Jesus comes, Jesus comes!
  Hallelujah, etc.

God with trumpet-tongue is speaking,
    Jesus comes, Jesus comes!
Souls are for a Saviour seeking,
    Jesus comes, Jesus comes!
  Hallelujah, etc.

Happy day is dawning o'er us,
    Jesus comes, Jesus comes!
Bright the way appears before us,
    Jesus comes, Jesus comes!
  Hallelujah, etc.

II.

Crowds before the cross are kneeling,
　　Jesus saves, Jesus saves!
By his boundless love revealing,
　　Jesus saves, Jesus saves!
　Hallelujah, light is beaming,
　Hallelujah, blood is streaming,
Hallelujah, hallelujah, Jesus saves!

All the lost and all the lonely
　　Jesus saves, Jesus saves!
Oh come now, believing only
　　Jesus saves, Jesus saves!
　Hallelujah, etc.

Hearts are at this moment proving
　　Jesus saves, Jesus saves!
Every sinful stain removing,
　　Jesus saves, Jesus saves!
　Hallelujah, etc.

Come with tears your sin confessing,
　　Jesus saves, Jesus saves!
Seek and find the choicest blessing,
　　Jesus saves, Jesus saves!
　Hallelujah, etc.

Hallelujah, saints are singing,
　　Jesus saves, Jesus saves!
Heaven with joyous song is ringing,
　　Jesus saves, Jesus saves!
　Hallelujah, etc.

THE KING'S ARMY.

" They all hold swords."

Christ Jesus is our Saviour King,
    Hallelujah!
Beneath his flag we fight and sing,
    Hallelujah, Hallelujah!
Every soldier holds a sword,
In the army of the Lord,
    Singing Hallelujah,
We are marching home, home, sweet home,
There to lay the sword and the armor down:
We are marching home, home, sweet home,
To share with our Saviour his royal crown.

The ranks of sin are falling fast,
    Hallelujah!
And Christ shall overcome at last,
    Hallelujah, Hallelujah!
Half the army's in the air,
Fighting o'er us everywhere,
    Singing hallelujah,
We are marching home, etc.

The world is bowing to our King,
    Hallelujah!
And prisoners of his love now sing,
    Hallelujah, hallelujah!
Thousands from the haunts of sin
To our rank are coming in,
    Singing hallelujah,
We are marching home, etc.

WATCHFULNESS.

"Every man hath his sword upon his thigh because of fear in the night."

Christian, watch when night is nigh,
Gird the sword upon the thigh;
Foes who fear the morning light
May o'ercome thee in the night.

Clouds of darkness will surround
Every soul that's heavenward bound;
And the purest fight their way
To the light of endless day.

Watch! for when no clouds appear
Night and danger may be near;
When the least prepared for strife,
We may lose the crown of life.

Watch! the sword is laid aside
Only when we cross the tide;
And a life of rest is given
When we reach the gates of heaven.

HOLDING ON TO JESUS.

"I held him, and would not let him go."

Holding on to Jesus, with the crown in sight,
Holding on to Jesus in the dark and light;
Though the world may tempt me with its luring
    dross,
Holding on to Jesus, clinging to the cross.

If I hold to Jesus, Jesus holds to me,
And each path of duty plainly can I see;
Over all I triumph, and secure abide,
Holding on to Jesus, clinging to his side.

Ere you can unshaken to the Saviour hold,
Earth must be forsaken, self and love of gold;
Gladly you must suffer every earthly loss,
Holding on to Jesus, clinging to the cross.

Bid farewell to pleasure, let the idols fall,
And the Saviour only be your all in all;
Nothing shall disturb you, though the tempests toss,
Holding on to Jesus, clinging to the cross.

SPOTLESS.

"There is no spot in thee."

THERE rests on my soul not a shadow or stain,
For Jesus hath washed me again and again;
His blood every moment doth over me flow,
Washing and keeping me whiter than snow.
   No spot is in thee,
   Says the Saviour to me,
   And true 'tis I know,
For what can be whiter than whiter than snow?

The world says that sin lieth still in my breast;
But Christ says I'm spotless — I'm sure he knows best:
I'll sing of that blood now, wherever I go,
Washing and keeping me whiter than snow.
   No spot is in thee, etc.

All glory to Jesus! all praise to the Lamb!
Through whose boundless mercy now spotless I
    am:
His blood all my journey is ever I know
Washing and keeping me whiter than snow.
        No spot is in thee, etc.

WAITING NEAR THE CROSS.

"Until the day break and the shadows flee away, I will get me to the mountains of myrrh and to the hill of frankincense."

Doubting hearts around us strive to lead astray
Those who seek salvation by the narrow way;
Scorn they cast on Jesus, trifle with his word,
Say that prayer in heaven is answered not nor
    heard.
        Near the cross I'm waiting,
            Safe from doubts and fears,
        Near the cross I'm waiting,
            Till the dawn appears.

Though we see but darkly, what a glorious sight
Will unfold before us in the morning light!
On this holy mountain, with love's odor sweet,
Safe my soul is resting, at the Saviour's feet.
        Near the cross, etc.

Art or science never can salvation test,
Comes its sweet revealing when in Christ we rest;
Light of reason cannot to the world impart
How a blessing enters to a praying heart.
        Fear the cross, etc.

LOOK AWAY TO JESUS.

"Look from the top of Amana, from the top of Shenir and Hermon, from the lions' den, from the mountains of the leopards."

Look away to Jesus, if you would be blest;
Looking at your weakness cannot give you rest;
And when full of faith, you keep the cross in view,
The Lord looks on Jesus, and not upon you.
  Look away to Jesus,
   He doth pardon give;
  Look away to Jesus,
   Oh look now and live!

Look away to Jesus when the clouds appear,
Look away to Jesus when the tempter's near;
And though seas of sorrow lift their mighty waves,
Look away to Jesus with a look that saves.
  Look away, etc.

Look away to Jesus! in the dark and light
Keep the cross of Jesus ever more in sight;
Every hour temptation plays its luring part,
Look away to Jesus, with a trusting heart.
  Look away, etc.

THE POWER OF ONE PURE HEART.

"Thou hast ravished my heart with one of thine eyes."

One pure heart shall move a mountain,
 Bid love's banner be unfurled,
Open wide the cleansing fountain
 To a nation or a world.

Let the prayer of Luther thunder,
    Crashing through the brassy skies;
And we shall behold the wonder
    Of a reformation rise.

Heaven cannot withstand the pleading
    Of a heart that sinneth not,
Nor the mighty interceding
    Of a church without a spot.

One pure heart shall shield a nation
    From the famine, blast, and rod;
And that fearful desolation
    Sweeping from an angry God.

In the word of God 'tis written,
    Truth by all the holy known,
Heart of Christ is sweetly smitten
    By a heart pure like his own.

THE ACCEPTABLE OFFERING.

"How much better is thy love than wine, and the smell of thine ointment than the smell of wine."

Nothing can such joy impart
To the Saviour's loving heart,
As that life his blood has bought
To his feet an offering brought:
Glad he welcomes to the throne
Love re-kindled by his own.

"Victory!" the angels cry,
When a soul to Christ draws nigh;
While across the crystal sea
Floats the voice of Calvary,
Telling through the heavens wide
How the Lord for sinners died.

Knowing all thy love to me,
Lord, I bring myself to thee;
Thou for me didst all resign,
Therefore all I have is thine:
To my soul thy life impart
While I give to thee my heart.

THE WORK OF LOVE.

"Thy lips, O my spouse, drop as the honeycomb; honey and milk are under thy tongue, and the smell of thy garments is like the smell of Lebanon."

O LOVE divine! what glories shine
Upon this ransomed heart of mine:
How sweet to rest upon thy breast,
And with thy smile be ever blest!
  Sweet was the hour, O Jesus!
  I felt thy power, O Jesus!
   Now I rest
   On thy breast
  Evermore, my Jesus!

When sorrow-tried, I safely hide
Within thy deeply riven side;
And shades of fear nor doubt appear
While thou to me, my Lord, art near.
  Sweet was the hour, etc.

With pure delight, in garments white,
I walk with Jesus in the light;
And all the while, in pain and trial,
I feel my loving Saviour's smile.
      Sweet was the hour, etc.

His love hath brought the rest I sought
In all its fulness, passing thought;
His head bowed low, his blood did flow
That I might full salvation know.
      Sweet was the hour, etc.

THE ENCLOSED GARDEN.

"A garden enclosed is my sister, my spouse; a spring shut up, a fountain sealed."

A GARDEN sweet, enclosed, secure,
  Art thou, O Zion dear!
Where all the holy, good, and pure
  In loveliness appear.

Amidst the world, and yet apart
  From all its angry strife,
The Saviour holds thee in his heart,
  And feeds thee with his life.

The hands which built the worlds above,
  And the eternal throne,
Thy temples reared by strength of love
  In sadness and alone.

From Edom, lonely, forth there came,
    With garments crimson dyed,
One who endured the cross and shame,
    Thorn-crown and wounded side,

That in this world of strife and sin,
    Thy gates be open thrown;
Where all who will may enter in
    To live for God alone.

THE PLANTS AND PLEASANT FRUITS.

"Thy plants are an orchard of pomegranates, with pleasant fruits."

HERE the tender plants are cherished,
    Here the pleasant fruit appears;
All the canker sins have perished
    Which did waste in former years.

Now the branches, upward tending,
    Catch the light and dews which fall;
Then to earth, well-laden, bending,
    Pleasant fruit refreshes all.

From the orchard winds are blowing
    For all wounded hearts a balm;
From this orchard, streams are flowing
    To all troubled hearts, with calm.

Winds are sent, through chambers stealing
    As a flower-breath from above;
To the dying saint unsealing
    Odors sweet from wounded love.

All the plants and trees are sharing
  Life, through Christ's redeeming plan;
And the fruit each tree is bearing
  Feeds the life divine in man.

THE FOUNTAIN.

"A fountain of gardens, a well of living waters, and streams from Lebanon."

Streams of grace forever flow
Through the Church of God below;
Nothing withers, nothing wanes,
For the Lord himself sustains
With a pure, life-giving flood,
All the purchase of his blood.

Without money, without price,
Life to all the Lord supplies;
And his streams of mercy flow
For the high and for the low;
All who need may be supplied
At this fountain, opened wide.

They who drink ne'er thirst again;
They who wash lose every stain;
To the dark it giveth light;
To the blind it giveth sight;
And eternal life imparts
To a world of weary hearts.

BLOW, SPIRIT, BLOW!

"Awake, O north wind, and come thou south; blow upon my garden, that the spices thereof may flow out."

O Spirit of God! in thy power sweep by,
And brighten the blossoms that sicken to die;
New life to my garden of beauty impart,
That spices may flow from each purified heart.
    O blow, Spirit, blow,
      And let the spices flow
When my Beloved shall pass this way.

I would to my Jesus a pure offering make
Of love's sweetest odors, for dying love's sake;
His wounded hands planted my garden so sweet,
And all that is best I would lay at his feet.
    O blow, Spirit, etc.

He's coming with angels robed whiter than snow,
My garden must bloom and my spices must flow;
He's coming to gather the fruit of that pain
He bore on the cross for the world and its stain.
    O blow, Spirit, etc.

WELCOME TO JESUS.

"Let my beloved come into his garden and eat his pleasant fruits."

Open wide opposing gates,
Christ to enter, knocking, waits;
He shall view with great delight
Ripened fruit and blossom white;
Smile to see no tree around
Fruitless, cumbering the ground.

For his church in by-gone years
He has shed his blood and tears,
That from cross of pain might spring
A divine and glorious thing.
Every gate be opened wide,
Welcome in the Crucified.

Jesus comes this day to feast
With the lowliest and the least;
Here with him in converse sweet
Fruit of love we all may eat;
While the Lord himself imparts
Light and joy to waiting hearts.

THE SPIRIT AND THE BRIDE.

Chapter v. 11.

I.

Oh where is my lost love? why doth she hide
  Her face from me for evermore?
I am thy Lord, and thou art my true Bride:
  I'm weary knocking at thy door.

Awake, awake, my love! why sleep so sound?
  Sorrow for thee is in my halls;
I will no more return till thou art found:
  Arise, come now, thy Saviour calls!

Long have I sought thee sorrowing; my hair
  Is wet with night dews, and my feet
Are weary; O my beloved, my fair
  One, come! and let us once more meet.

My father is not angry now; alone
   I trod the winepress, bore his ire
For thee; my sorrow makes thee more mine own,
   Thy presence my heart's best desire.

II.

Call me not bride; the bridal robes thou gavest me
   Are all defiled, sin-stained; the beauteous flowers
Thy hands placed on my brow, they are not fair to see
   As when I wore them first in Eden's bowers.

Death follows my footsteps evermore, and time
   Writes deepening wrinkles on my limbs and brow;
The earth is not as of old a sinless clime,—
   Thou wouldst not know me if thou sawest me now.

Thou art all holiness, but I am all sin;
   Thou art most lovely, I am old and gray;
Decay is on me, my spirit dark within;
   I weep, but tears wash not my guilt away.

I heard thy heavenly voice of plaintive tone
   Calling upon me in my fearful sleep;
And dreamed a moment I was again thine own,
   With brow more beautiful and love more deep.

THE SPIRIT AND THE BRIDE.

Alas, Lord, it is not so, and never more
    Can I walk spotless, sinless, at thy side;
I am not worthy to open thee the door,
    I am a fallen star, and not thy bride.

III.

I know thy bridal robes are broken, but I have woven new;
I know the vows thou gavest me of old, thou hast not kept them true;
Yet still within my heart for thee is the love which once it bore;
The bridegroom that loveth once his bride, loveth her evermore.

The wrinkles which o'er thy limbs are spread, the shadows on thy brow,
Shall vanish away when thou vowest again thy former vow;
For thee my side was pierced, for thee my hands with nails were torn,
On me thy weight of guilt was cast, and my soul was made to mourn.

Now let the false idols thou hast loved be all shattered at thy feet,
And turn again to my bosom, and thy rest shall be long and sweet;
And thou shalt sicken no more 'neath a dead love's withering breath,
Nor sit in garments of sorrow, nor look again upon death.

And thou shalt walk with sinless soul ever at thy
 true love's side,
To be more lovely and more loved than when
 thou wast first his bride;
For the past shall never more rise with dark
 wings over thy sight,
But round about and o'er thee, shall be heaven
 and all its light.

IV.

I am o'erwhelmed with grief, my Lord, to think
 on all thou hast borne
For me; thine agony and bloody sweat, limbs
 so bruised and torn;
And that thou, the fairest of all on earth, or in
 heaven above,
Shouldst bear for me still in thy bosom so beauti-
 ful a love.
Nothing have I to give thee, my Lord, nothing
 have I to bring;
Lo, at thy feet, I sorrowing fall, a mean and
 worthless thing;
And here will I cling for evermore close to thy
 bleeding side,
For thou hast called me again thy love, called me
 again thy bride.
I feel, as I nearer draw to thee, look on thy ra-
 diant brow,
Those dark thoughts vanish away that haunted
 my soul until now;
While the rags from my limbs fall off, all the
 filthy rags of sin,
And I am arrayed in white without, and full of
 light within.

Bend over me now with a smile, and tell me I am forgiven,
And give me the kiss of love that lifts the soul from earth to heaven;
Oh fold around me thy wounded hands, let me lie upon thy breast,
Where the wicked cease from troubling, and the weary are at rest!

v.

Awake, O harp! with a lofty strain,
   Heaven's gates be opened wide!
The Bridegroom nears the eternal spheres,
   And he bringeth home his Bride.

She is robed in all that is rare,
   There's a new light in her eye;
We strew her way to eternal day
   With flowers that never die.

Oh how he loved her! and how he wept
   To see she had sunk so low;
To see his Bride fall from his side
   To the deepest depths of woe!

But his step is light and joyous now,
   And his lips are bright with smiles,
Telling his love of the joy above
   Here in the heavenly isles.

Lift up your heads, O ye golden gates!
   And eternal doors swing wide!
The King of glory to enter waits,
   With his newly-ransomed Bride.

THE SORROWS OF SIN.

"The watchmen that went about the city found me; they smote me, they wounded me."

I.

The Word which once so soothing came
Now smites me like a scorching flame;
The sabbath bell, the voice of praise,
Wound with the joys of better days.

The name of Jesus, once so dear,
Now fills my heart with shame and fear;
The mention of his thorny crown
Reveals the love I trampled down.

Of what I am I dare not think,
And from the thought of dying shrink;
The path of duty once I trod,
But now am far from light and God.

Though I have wounded Jesus so,
My heart received the fiercest blow;
And all my joy to grief is turned
Through pity of that love I spurned.

II.

O Jesus, hear my cry!
 A poor lost child of thine:
In answer to my prayer draw nigh,
 And take this load of mine.

Long years this heavy weight
  Of sins I've sadly borne;
But now heart-broken, desolate,
  I to thy feet return.

O Jesus! let me in
  To thy sweet rest of love;
And I no more will stoop to sin,
  But rise to joys above.

I cannot bear this load,
  I faint by guilt oppressed:
Shine out upon the darksome road,
  And guide me to thy rest.

SEEKING A LOST SAVIOUR.

"I opened to my beloved, but my beloved had withdrawn himself and was gone; I sought him, but I could not find him; I called him, but he gave me no answer."

The light of the Lord from my path is withdrawn,
The peace of my spirit is broken and gone;
I call, but he answers me not as of old;
I've wandered away from the track of the fold.

It was but a moment I trifled, and lo,
The stains on that garment once whiter than snow;
A sigh for the idols I knew must depart,
And Jesus went out at the door of my heart.

I promised to give up the things I loved best,
If Jesus would come to my bosom and rest;
No idol should ask for a share in his throne,
And nothing delight me but Jesus alone.

That promise is broken, the Saviour has fled;
The blossoms of love are all withered and dead;
The clouds have o'ershadowed the brightness of dawn,
I'm alone in the dark, and Jesus is gone.

THE CHIEFEST.

"The chiefest among ten thousand."

Through the strength of love divine
Jesus ever first shall shine;
Universe of spirits bright
Pale before his fuller light:
He my chiefest love shall be,
Who hath shed his blood for me.

Prince of princes, king of kings!
Glory of all glorious things;
Whom the highest evermore
Feel it blessed to adore:
He the chiefest joy I know,
For he washed me white as snow.

He shall be my chiefest stay,
All along the heavenly way;
He shall be my chiefest trust
When this mortal turns to dust:
He my chiefest love shall be,
Now, and in eternity.

THE ALTOGETHER LOVELY.

"He is altogether lovely."

How lovely is Jesus, the Lamb that was slain,
To win a world's pardon by sorrow and pain;
How lovely that crown on his once bleeding brow,
And lovely his love which o'ershadows me now!

Oh! lovely, surpassing all loveliness, he,
Who died with the thief for a lost world and me,
That all might be perfected here by his love,
And meet him with white robes in heaven above.

How lovely that life, doing good everywhere!
How lovely that death, with its merciful prayer!
And lovely that blood which on Calvary flowed,
When it washes the heart and lightens its load.

How lovely is Jesus, when close to his side,
From doubt and temptation securely we hide!
And lovely his presence, when loving him best,
He comes to our hearts with the blessing of rest.

GATHERED LILIES.

"My beloved is gone down into his garden, . . . to gather lilies."

I.

We mourn the loss of one whose days
Were spent in duty, prayer, and praise;
The cross he nobly bore, and now
A crown of glory decks his brow.

He early sought the narrow way,
And humbly walked it day by day;
His death the blessed verdict gave
That Jesus' blood can fully save.

Though ours the loss and his the gain,
His memory fragrant will remain;
And lessons from his wisdom drawn
Will bless us still, though he is gone.

No more his voice in prayer or praise
Will cheer us, as in other days;
But through the grace our God supplies
We soon shall meet him in the skies.

II.

O God! our strength and shield,
  Be near us while we mourn
One fallen on the battle-field,
  And to his slumber borne.

He fought for Jesus well,
  In stern and holy strife;
At post of duty nobly fell,
  And rose to endless life.

Who shall his standard bear,
  For Christ and heaven unfurled?
Who wrestle with his strength in prayer
  For blessings on the world.

O God! our strength and shield,
  Support us in this hour:
To all who mourn be Christ revealed,
  With sweet, consoling power.

We lay him in the tomb,
   Until God's angel flies
From heaven to earth, with trump of doom,
   And all the dead shall rise.

We lay him down to rest,
   A brother true and dear;
With all whom Jesus loved the best
   He shall in bliss appear.

III.

Gone across the mystic river,
   To the Eden shore;
Safe with God and Christ forever,
   To return no more.

Gone, though lying now before us
   In a slumber deep;
Safe in heavenly mansions o'er us,
   Never more to weep.

Gone: the pain and toil are ended,
   Finished all the strife;
For the spirit hath ascended
   To eternal life.

Gone the weakness and the sighing,
   Changing hopes and fears;
Gone the weariness of dying,
   And the blinding tears.

Gone across the mystic river,
   One more gathered home;
Safe with God and Christ forever,
   Waiting till we come.

IV.

Softly let the music swell,
As we sing a long farewell,
Look our last on one whose rest
Tells how sweetly sleep the blest:
Breathe a prayer on every breath,
For how near we are to death!

In the stillness so profound
God himself seems walking round;
Telling in the silence deep,
Blest are they who fall asleep,
All the work assigned them done,
Trusting in his blessed Son.

Softly let the music swell,
As we sing farewell, farewell!
Never more on earth we meet
To engage in worship sweet.
Till we stand where angels dwell,
Sing we now farewell, farewell!

V.

Where the sound of human voices
  Fall not on the raptured ear,
The unfettered soul rejoices
  In a brighter, holier sphere.

Never more can sorrow sadden,
  Care be an abiding guest;
For all that is bright doth gladden,
  In the spirit's heavenly rest.

Doubt no more can bring suggestion,
    Wounding faith in heavenward flight;
For each deep and shadowed question
    Shines out in the clearest light.

Christ with balm is sweetly healing
    All the wounds the spirit bore;
And of life and love revealing
    Deeper depths for ever more.

VI.

He sleeps, so loved and mourned by those
    Who heard him teach with purpose strong
The way to win a heaven's repose,
    By seeking right and shunning wrong.

He sleeps so peacefully, that now
    The labor of his life is o'er,
A smile of rest falls on his brow,
    Which care or pain can shade no more.

He sleeps, like all the good and just
    Who nobly fall in holy strife,
With a sublime and humble trust
    In the eternal, after life.

He sleeps, and that great weight of pain
    Which bowed his soul to shades of night,
Can touch him not, nor cloud again,
    Up in that world of perfect light.

VII.

Early, early called away
In the midst of childhood's play,
To rejoin on Canaan's shore
Playmates that have gone before:
Leaving others to prepare
For their change, and meet her there.

Early, early this for flight
To the world of mansions bright;
Early to be homeward bound,
Early to be victor crowned;
Early this to join above
Choirs that sing redeeming love.

Though so early, this we know,
Jesus washed her white as snow;
He who once the children blest
Brought her safe to shores of rest:
Though so early, child, thou hast
All life's danger safely passed.

VIII.

With loving hands we bear to rest,
    And yield the tribute of our tears,
The dead, whose memory will be blest
    To many hearts, through future years.

The tongue on which death's seal is set
    Hath filled this house with praise and prayer,
And years must pass ere we forget
    The loving words it uttered here.

Where oft it knelt for bread and wine
  The body lies, removed from strife;
The features seeming more divine
  Than through the years of holy life.

We learn amidst this solemn scene
  A holy life alone is blest;
That Jesus' blood can wash us clean,
  And purchase everlasting rest.

We part where grief is deep and long,
  And nothing can our tears restrain;
We meet at last, with shout and song,
  When Jesus comes to earth again.

SHE COMETH AS THE MORNING.

She cometh as the morning, clear as the sun,
  And she neareth her noonday splendor;
For the holy light of the crucified One
  Doth in all her journey attend her.

She cometh as the morning, with light and song,
  Wearing garments of snowy whiteness;
And all by the way where she passes along
  She sheddeth her blessings and brightness.

She cometh as the morning, quenching the night
  Of burdensome doubt and of sadness;
She giveth unto faith a garment of white,
  And to all her followers gladness.

She cometh as the morning, and all shall see
　By the light which her Lord hath given,
That the spirit must perfect and holy be
　Before it can pass into heaven.

RESTING UNAWARES.

"Or ever I was aware my soul made me like the chariots of Ammi-nadib."

Or ever I was aware, before the Saviour's feet,
Through the depths of love divine, my soul found
　　blessings sweet;
When feeling my weariness most, and darkest
　　fell the night,
Or ever I was aware, there came a flood of light.

Through wearisome, doubting years, my soul had
　　been in quest
Of higher walks of being, and deeper depths of
　　rest;
But seeing a wounded side, touching a wounded
　　palm,
Or ever I was aware, there came a wondrous
　　calm.

And I found my faith awake, her clear eye fixed
　　above,
With a rapture drinking in the light of perfect
　　love;
While over my melting heart a purer will did
　　dawn,
Or ever I was aware, my wayward will was gone.

Though long be the way we seek, suddenly light
    will fall,
The moment we leave ourselves, and Christ is
    all in all;
The moment we break away from things we love
    the best,
Or ever we are aware, we reach the mount of
    rest.

WHO IS SHE THAT LOOKETH FORTH AS THE MORNING?

"Who is she that looketh forth as the morning, fair as the moon, clear as the sun, and terrible as an army with banners?"

Who is she that looketh out upon the darkness
    of the world,
Like the coming of an army with its banners all
    unfurled?
With a fuller glory round her than the brightest
    morn can show,
And her garments flowing whiter than the whitest
    driven snow?
'Tis the coming of the Church of God most high!
    Hallelujah!
For Jesus hath washed her in his blood all white,
And sent her to spread in lines of golden light,
That he for the love of a lost world did die,
    Hallelujah, hallelujah!
      Fair as the moon,
        Clear as the sun,
      To holiness soon
        The world will be won.

Who is she that cometh bearing in her hand a
    cross of light,
And an overflowing fountain that doth wash the
    sinner white?
With a voice that wakes the sleeper and a look
    that wins the lost,
Giving peace to all the weary on a sea of sorrow
    tossed?
'Tis the coming of the Church, etc.

Who is this that cometh bearing precious prom-
    ises of love,
To a world that lies in darkness from a world of
    light above?
With the means for the renewal and the washing
    white as snow
Of all them that trust in Jesus and unto the foun-
    tain go?
'Tis the coming of the Church, etc.

LIFT ME UP, O JESUS!

"This thy stature is like a palm-tree. . . . I said, I will go up to the palm-tree, I will take hold of the boughs thereof."

Lift me up, O Jesus! higher still and higher,
Till I lose the thraldom of each low desire;
Let thy cross of glory only hold my heart,
And the perfect fulness of thy love impart.

Lift me up, O Jesus! to the fuller light,
Where the cloudless sunshine falls upon the sight;
Where this painful fearing shall forever cease,
In the full enjoyment of thy perfect peace.

Lift me up, O Jesus! nearer, nearer thee,
Where my restless longings all at rest shall be ;
Where mine eye beholding form of love divine,
There may come a moulding of my will to thine.

Lift me up, O Jesus! higher still, and higher,
Seraphim, fly swiftly, touch my lips with fire!
That while God is calling, who will servant be?
All my soul may answer, here am I ; send me !

GOING FORTH WITH JESUS.

"Come, my beloved, let us go forth into the field; let us lodge in the villages."

Going forth with Jesus, leaving doubts and fears,
Trusting but in Jesus all my future years ;
Hearing his voice only, counting all but loss
For the cleansing virtue of the wondrous cross.
 I am going forth with Jesus,
  To publish day and night,
 That the precious blood of Jesus
  Can wash and keep us white :
 That the precious blood of Jesus
  Shall fill the world with light.

Going forth with Jesus, breaking all the ties
That would hold my spirit from the heavenly
 prize ;
Loving only Jesus, knowing but his own,
Parting with all pleasures for the cross alone.
 I am going forth with Jesus, etc.

Going forth with Jesus, oh how sweet the way!
To be his companion every happy day;
Hearing his voice morning, noon; and through
    the night
Feeling he waits near me till the dawning light.
    I am going forth with Jesus, etc.

Going forth with Jesus, telling where I go
How the blood of Jesus washed me white as snow;
How each day it keeps me free from sinful stains,
While o'er all my being, Jesus only reigns.
    I am going forth with Jesus, etc.

Going forth with Jesus, he my guide shall be,
Till I pass the valley, to the crystal sea;
Then with angel harpers, in a world of light,
I will tell how Jesus washed my garments white.
    I am going forth with Jesus, etc.

LEANING ON THE ARM OF JESUS.

"Who is this that cometh up from the wilderness leaning upon her beloved?"

We are coming up out
  Of the wilderness of doubt,
    Leaning on the arm of Jesus;
We are pressing our way
  To the fuller light of day,
    Leaning on the arm of Jesus.
That blessing is the deepest, purest, and best,
  The blood which from bondage frees us;
That rest is the sweetest of all earthly rest,
  Leaning on the arm of Jesus.

We are fearing no foe,
As to higher joys we go,
    Leaning on the arm of Jesus;
And the love of our God
In each heart is shed abroad,
    Leaning on the arm of Jesus.
That blessing, etc.

With our garment of white,
We are walking in the light,
    Leaning on the arm of Jesus;
And we never can stray,
Or be lost along the way,
    Leaning on the arm of Jesus.
That blessing, etc.

We have nothing to bear,
For we lose the weight of care,
    Leaning on the arm of Jesus;
And our fulness of peace,
Shall evermore increase,
    Leaning on the arm of Jesus.
That blessing, etc.

OTHER POEMS.

OTHER POEMS.

HYMNS ON THE TRANSFIGURATION.

HOLY FEAR.

"And they feared as they entered into the cloud."

The three disciples feared to walk
   With Jesus where he led,
And trembled when they heard him talk
   With men they knew were dead.

They feared the cloud which only brought
   A glory from the skies,
That in their natures might be wrought,
   The life which never dies.

So when the voice of Jesus rings,
   And glory round us rolls,
We fear the very cloud that brings
   The blessings to our souls.

All ye who long for perfect love,
   Which doubt nor fear can shroud,
By faith rise to that mount above
   And pass into the cloud.

Fear not, and you shall now be blest,
   With heart and soul made clean,
And live a life of perfect rest
   Where Christ alone is seen.

TRANSFORMING POWER OF PRAYER.

"And as he prayed the fashion of his countenance was altered, and his raiment was white and glistering."

As Jesus humbly bowed in prayer,
   His raiment changed to white,
The fashion of his face more fair
   Than all the sons of light.

So when in prayer we humbly kneel,
   The mercy-seat in view,
A change doth o'er our spirits steal,
   And we are wrought anew.

When guilt and sin our hearts confess,
   With sorrow most profound,
The robe of Jesus' righteousness
   Doth sweetly fold us round.

Though shade of sin could never be
   On life of Christ so fair,
He taught us in the mount, how we
   May be transformed by prayer.

TALKING OF CALVARY.

"And spake of his decease which he should accomplish at Jerusalem."

To the mount of holy flame
Moses and Elias came
From their rest in light above,
To behold incarnate Love,
Talk of bloody conflict nigh,
When the Lord himself should die.

Wondering they beheld the man
Who should end redemption's plan,
That divine one whom they saw
Through the shadows of the law;
Now the dawning age of grace
Shone out from the Saviour's face.

Could he bear the thorny crown?
Could he dare the Father's frown?
Would his mighty love prevail
O'er the wound of spear and nail?
So they talked of his decease,
While the answers gave them peace.

Love so deep, so broad, and high,
Full a thousand times could die;
Though two worlds and hell should frown,
He could wear the thorny crown.
While they talked, the Saviour's face
Changed, and glory filled the place.

JESUS ONLY.

"And when they lifted up their eyes, they saw no man save Jesus only."

When the three disciples bowed
On the mount beneath the cloud,
Glory swept them through and through,
Drifting former things from view,
And by perfect love set free,
Jesus only could they see.

Prophets clad in raiment bright,
Sank before the greater light;
This is my beloved Son,
Spake the high and holy one;
Gazing there, on bended knee,
Jesus only could they see.

When upon the mount we go,
'Neath the glory bending low,
Near the blood besprinkled throne,
Talk with Jesus all alone,
Every cloud of doubt must flee,
Jesus only shall we see.

Jesus only be our light,
And the pathway must be bright;
Jesus only seen and felt,
Every cloud of doubt shall melt;
Jesus only be our stay,
Safe we reach eternal day.

GOOD TO BE HERE.

"It is good for us to be here."

How blest this hour, how passing sweet,
To gather round the mercy-seat,
And offer praise to him whose smile
Transfigures all our souls the while.

Here on the mount with Christ alone,
We see the grandeur of his throne,
And lost in glory from above
Drink in the fulness of his love.

Here would we build, and here abide,
With prophets at the Saviour's side,
Here on the mount would spend our days,
Till lost in everlasting praise.

Not yet for us the mansion bright;
We leave the mount to join the fight,
And win, by doing each his best,
The mount of everlasting rest.

CLOSET SONGS.

SHUT IN.

"When thou prayest, enter into thy closet."

Shut in with Jesus, oh how sweet
The silence of this calm retreat!
Here, while I meditate and pray,
All doubt and darkness flee away;
And through the sky the prayer-perfume
Floats from the censer to my room.

Shut in with Jesus, here a while
Bathed in the sunshine of his smile,
My soul is lost in visions bright
Of that sweet country out of sight;
For faith doth cull its fadeless bloom,
And with the fragrance fill my room.

Shut in with Jesus, as I kneel
He doth his wondrous love reveal:
And resting on each promise sweet
I lay my burdens at his feet;
While from my room across the tide,
I see the heavens opened wide.

Shut in with Jesus, here I learn
What things to cherish, what to spurn;
How in this world of fading light
To keep the better world in sight,
And yield the things that please me best
To gain my everlasting rest.

THE CLOSET HOUR.

There is a time when God's great word,
 Falls o'er my heart with cleansing power,
And all my soul to prayer is stirred,—
 It is the hallowed closet hour.

No sound of strife doth e'er invade,
 Nor any earthly joy possess
The holy calm which doth pervade
 A heart that waits for God to bless.

Oh closet hour, thou dost reveal
 God's judgment and his mercy sweet,
And lead me as a child to kneel
 Submissive at the Saviour's feet.

Thou dost impart new life and strength
 Unto my soul, and I can see
The depth and height, the breadth and length
 Of Christ's amazing love for me.

With thee the Saviour comes and brings
 Divine revealings, old and new;
And all that feast of heavenly things
 He sweetly hallows, feasting too.

O closet hour, O wealth of days!
　O calm like that the heavens wear!
Come often, till I thrill with praise
　The harp that now is tuned to prayer.

AWAY TO THE MERCY-SEAT.

"He went away and prayed."

Away from the hum of the crowded street,
　　The grip of money-mart,
Away to the calm of the mercy-seat,
Where all that is holy, divine, and sweet
　　Falls round the weary heart.

Away in the morn ere labors begin,
　　Devoutly read and pray,
That the Christ of God to thy heart come in,
And keep it untouched by the blight of sin
　　Through all the toilsome day.

Away when the bustle of toil has fled,
　　With heart o'erflowing tell
Thy thanks for a bountiful table spread,
For the strength of heart and the strength of head
　　To do thy duty well.

Away to the closet when bright hopes flee,
　　And eyes with tears grow dim;
For a Saviour prayed in Gethsemane,
And the angels will come to strengthen thee
　　As the angel strengthened him.

THREE TIMES A DAY.

"Evening, and morning, and at noon will I pray."

Three times a day
Did prophets pray :
Am I purer, Lord, than they?
Daniel dared the lions' den,
Would not yield to sinful men,
And though but an exile's son
Rose the first in Babylon.
He did pray
Three times a day.

From the fiercely-heated flame
The three Hebrews safely came ;
With them through the furnace trod
One like to the Son of God.
They did pray
Three times a day.

David from the harp hath flung
Rhymeless gems for every tongue,
And though born to tend a fold,
Kingly wore a crown of gold.
He did pray
Three times a day.

Holy men who loved God's Word
Stood the test of fire and sword,
And in dying left behind
Bright examples for mankind.
They did pray
Three times a day :
Am I purer, Lord, than they?

CAST ME NOT AWAY FROM THY PRESENCE.

By the weight of guilt oppressed,
Lord, I come to thee for rest;
Only strength of love divine
Can remove this load of mine:
From thy presence while I pray,
Jesus, cast me not away.

Dark, — my soul is dark within,
Shadowed by the curse of sin;
Dark the road I've wandered o'er,
Dark the pathway on before;
From thy presence, where is day,
Jesus, cast me not away.

Thou alone canst light my road,
Thou alone canst take my load;
Only blood which thou hast spilt
Can remove the stains of guilt:
From thy presence while I pray,
Jesus, cast me not away.

SEEKING JESUS.

"Thy face, Lord, will I seek."

In the closet, all alone,
  Lord, I come to seek thy face;
While I make my longings known,
  With thy glory fill the place.

Give me strength of heart to bear
   Scorn of men and wound of creed,
And to preach thee everywhere,
   By the loving word and deed.

Thou hast all my weakness seen,
   Every sin in every place;
With thy precious blood make clean;
   Lord, for this I seek thy face.

Bathe my soul with light divine,
   Thou who art of light the fount,
That each thought and deed may shine
   With the glory of the Mount.

Give my faith a large increase,
   As thou dost thy face reveal;
Fill me with thy perfect peace
   While before thy feet I kneel.

May my soul with ravished sight
   Through the Word thy footsteps trace;
In the dark and in the light
   May I seek and see thy face!

WAITING ON THE LORD.

ABIDING here where righteousness
And peace each other sweetly kiss,
Where truth and mercy blend their rays
To gild the rising day of grace:
I see the central sun of love
Which lighteth all things from above,
      Waiting on the Lord.

The truths that were half hid from sight
Shine out in purer, clearer light;
The doubts that filled my soul with dread
Like mists before the sun have fled;
New strength to nobly work my part
In God's great plan, inspires my heart,
    Waiting on the Lord.

I learn how in this world of strife
To win the crown of endless life,
How swift the moments glide away
That hide from view the judgment-day;
And hear the ever deepening strain,
"All but the holy live in vain,"
    Waiting on the Lord.

I feel the calm of those who know
In whom they trust, and catch the glow
Of holy thought, and feel the rest
Prepared for those who love God best
Sink o'er my spirit, while each day
But clearer lights my heavenly way,
    Waiting on the Lord.

CAST THY BURDEN ON THE LORD.

Murmur not at sore oppressings,
  Cold neglect or angry word,
For our burdens turn to blessings
  When we cast them on the Lord.
This is why the grief is given,
  Wound from things we love the best,
That our spirits may be driven
  To a more enduring rest.

When the scenes of pleasure please us,
　For this world alone we live,
Then to bring us nearer Jesus
　God doth heavy burdens give.
When unholy lives are bringing
　To our hearts a sad reward,
Comes the voice of mercy ringing,
　"Cast thy burden on the Lord."

Not alone on sinful weakness
　Falls the crushing weight of care;
Those who bear the cross with meekness,
　Sorrow's burden too must bear.
This is how God brings us nearer
　To himself, day after day,
And our rest will be the dearer
　For the burdens by the way.

Some within their bosoms carry
　Wounds from Satan's poisoned sword;
Do not longer fearing tarry,
　Cast *yourselves* upon the Lord.
Jesus is our sorrow sharer,
　He hath suffered heart and limb;
Jesus is our burden bearer,
　Rest we all our weight on him.

PEACE.

"Peace," you know, was in the singing
　Which the shepherds heard that night
When the angels passed them, bringing
　Earthward, tidings of delight.

"Peace," you know, was in the greeting
  Which the lone disciples heard,
When into their evening meeting
  Came the newly risen Lord.

"Peace" it was that o'er the ocean
  Lashed to fury, sweetly rose;
And the waves amidst their motion
  Stood obedient in repose.

So that voice is still commanding,
  When the waves of sorrow roll,
Peace, that passeth understanding,
  To becalm the troubled soul.

THE PRISONER'S SIGH.

"Let the sighing of the prisoner come before thee."

Sighs from purer lips are winging
  Where the prayer and praises meet,
And the universe is bringing
  Worlds of glory to thy feet.
While the pure with pure are vying
  To applaud thy loving sway,
Lord, wilt hear my feeble sighing
  In this prison far away?

Bound by wasting chains of sickness
  From which death alone can free,
It would strengthen me in weakness
  To be heard in heaven by thee:

Hear and answer by revealing
  Why at noon the night should fall;
And the blessedness of feeling
  That thy love is over all.

Calm the tumult of my crying,
  As thou didst the angry sea;
Let the discord of my sighing
  Be as music sweet to thee.
May the sun of mercy risen,
  Risen ne'er to set again,
Shine upon me in this prison
  Till I praise thee for my pain!

LOVE'S QUESTION.

"Lovest thou me?" Ah, Lord, the wasted
  Hours of life doth plainly show,
And the pleasure I have tasted,
  Tasting still, all answer no.
Prayerless days and thoughtless actions,
  Promises that bloomed to die,
And the power of earth's attractions
  Give the terrible reply.

"Lovest thou me?" the faint resistance
  To each wrong I daily make,
And that shadow of assistance
  Given others for thy sake,
Smite me, as before thee kneeling,
  I would my devotion tell,
With the terrible revealing
  That I do not love thee well.

"Lovest thou me?" ah! why that question
　From love's lips to one loved so?
Why that withering suggestion
　From my heart to answer no?
Oh, the curse of idle living
　What can never be lived o'er!
Help me, by the past forgiving,
　Lord, to serve and love thee more.

TRUST IN GOD.

"Trust in Him at all times."

When success its pleasures bring,
　　　　　Trust in God.
When the clouds their shadows fling,
　　　　　Trust in God.
Through every scene, at every time,
In God repose a trust sublime.

When the children round thee play,
　　　　　Trust in God.
When death smites them into clay,
　　　　　Trust in God.
Though deep the sorrow, sharp the rod,
Let nothing shake thy trust in God.

Friends will leave when sorrows blight,
　　　　　Trust in God.
Wealth will take a sudden flight,
　　　　　Trust in God.
Let every idol turn to dust,
In God be evermore thy trust.

WORDS OF COMFORT.

There is a rest on Jesus' breast
  For all by weight of care oppressed,
And comfort sweet for them that meet
  In prayer around his mercy-seat.

There is a light to guide aright
  Unto that city, out of sight;
And none need stray, or miss their way,
  Who seek the world of perfect day.

There is a sweet and calm retreat,
  Where storms come not or tempests beat;
Its hallowed sod alone is trod
  By those who truly worship God.

GLORY TO THE NAZARENE.

Passing by each fading treasure,
Trump of fame and smile of pleasure,
    Going to the Nazarene,
Who for every earthly loss
Giveth gold unmixed with dross,
'Neath the shadow of the cross,
    Glory to the Nazarene.

Leaving philosophic questions,
And all skeptical suggestions,
    Thinking with the Nazarene.
Farewell, faithless, doubting years,
Farewell, trembling steps and tears,
Plain and sweet the way appears,
    Glory to the Nazarene.

Shut up in a sweet seclusion,
Angel forms the sole intrusion,
  Kneeling with the Nazarene;
Drifting on a sea of light,
Out of wrong into the right,
Out of weakness into might,
  Glory to the Nazarene.

Going to my daily calling,
Without thought or fear of falling,
  Walking with the Nazarene.
Ever since I learned to pray,
Every step along the way
Brightens to the perfect day,
  Glory to the Nazarene.

MORNING SONG.

The wild bird now from its nest is springing
Up to the cloudland, cheerily singing,
Making the universe ring with the story
Of God and his goodness, his greatness and glory.

Shall I, who have reason divine in me dwelling,
Go forth to my labor in silence, rebelling,
Not thanking that God who in darkness and slumber,
Watched over me, and his worlds without number?

If I ask for a blessing, God then will bestow it,
Though I hear not his voice nor see him, I know it;
By the pen of the prophet and saint he has spoken;
Not a promise of all he has made will be broken.

Then go forth, my song, with a far flight to heaven,
In a prayer that the sins of my soul be forgiven;
And though Satan may strive with his wiles and
    waylaying,
I am nobler for thanking and stronger for pray-
    ing.

I shall feel as I toil there is one far above me,
Who, though he may chasten, will watch o'er and
    love me,
And lead me at last to a land full of beauty,
From a sorrowing world, by the pathway of duty.

EVENING PSALM.

I would speak to thee, my Maker, now the day
    draws near its close,
While all nature and all being sinks into a deep
    repose.
In the shadows of the twilight, in the evenings'
    holy calm,
I would raise to thee, my Maker, all my worship
    in a psalm.

For the sin I have committed through this day of
    toil and care,
I ask thy blessed pardon, Lord, I ask it in a
    prayer.
Thou wilt not scorn a wayward child, that comes
    to thee, and brings
A broken and a wounded heart for shelter 'neath
    thy wings.

And let unnumbered blessings, Lord, this night
  around us fall,
Like dews which o'er the hills descend, enough
  for me and all.
Blessing cannot exhaust thy love, nor gifts thy
  boundless store,
We only have to praying take, and come again
  for more.

Be with the sailor tossed about, far on the path-
  less main;
Be with the soldier bivouack'd upon the battle-plain;
Pass through the lone, sick chamber, Lord, and
  lightens with thy smile
The lips that close forever more upon a world of
  trial.

I know thy name is merciful: the wrong that I
  have done,
Thou wilt forgive me when I pray, for Jesus is
  thy Son;
And though the angels round thy throne sing
  ever of thy worth,
Thou still wilt hear me when I plead, in this lone
  room on earth.

And Jesus values dearer far than strains which
  round him roll,
The accents rising heavenward from one repent-
  ing soul;
And dearer far, to his kind heart, than lay from
  harp of gold,
The bleating of a wandering lamb, without the
  heavenly fold.

LONGINGS.

Lord, to know thy gracious will,
   Is my every day endeavor,
And through good report and ill
   To be thine and thine forever.
Cleanse and purify my heart;
Let me never more depart
From the shadow of thy wings,
Hungering after earthly things.

Lead me to the fountain where
   My spirit may drink deep of thee;
In the solemn depths of prayer,
   Let me all thy glory see.
When on bended knee at morn,
Call me son, though lowly born;
When on bended knee at even,
Father, hear my prayer in heaven.

HYMN OF CONSECRATION.

O Master of the harvest fields! I pray
   Thee take me as a laborer of thine:
The pleasures of the world I cast away,
   And all its fleeting joys at once resign.

Take all my gifts, for thou hast given all;
   Take all my thought, from thee alone it came;
But oh! the offering seems so poor and small,
   I lay it at thy feet with fear and shame.

HYMN OF CONSECRATION.

Now on the altar cleanse the gift from dross;
   Send thy refining spirit from above,
That with clean hands I may take up the cross,
   And tell the story of the Saviour's love.

Without thy aid all work of man is vain;
   Thy hidden wisdom to my soul impart,
That I may speak the message clear and plain,
   With saving power to every wayward heart.

Help me to lead a blameless life below,
   That by example I may preach thy word;
And in the humblest duty ever show
   I'm walking in the footsteps of my Lord.

Give me a willing heart to undertake
   With earnest purpose every trying task,
Knowing that for our dear Redeemer's sake
   Thou wilt give more than I can think or ask.

More faith, when faith seems growing dim and weak;
   More strength, when prayer seems shorn of eagle wings;
And all my soul through faith in Christ shall seek
   Of heavenly meetness and of heavenly things.

Let every hour be usefully employed,
   Each day leave something finished or begun,
That no part of my life may be a void,
   With so much work for Jesus to be done.

Oh! make the study of the sacred page
   My chief delight, in sickness or in health;
And save me from the errors of the age,
   Its thirst for pleasure, and its race for wealth.

And when on sabbath day I lay thy Word
   Before the people, give it mighty power:
Let man be silent, God alone be heard,
   And bless thy vineyard with a gracious shower.

In every duty help me to be true;
   In every motive help me to be pure;
With cheerfulness my daily task pursue,
   With patience every trying cross endure.

If thou shouldst deem it wise and best to send
   Affliction, with its scourge, to me or mine,
Help me submissive 'neath thy rod to bend,
   And to thy hands what best I love resign.

And when at last before thy bar I stand,
   Through Jesus' merits be my sins forgiven;
Give me a place with saints at thy right hand,
   A happy home for evermore in heaven.

OBEDIENCE.

Oh! thou who didst with thine own blood
   The vengeance of the Father stay,
Inspire my heart with sacred love,
   Thy will in all things to obey.

When friends forsake and cares invade,
  'Tis sweet upon thy breast to lean,
And feel thy love is still the same,
  That through all time has changeless been.

The world is false, but thou art true;
  Beneath thy cross I rest secure:
The world is death, but thou art life;
  For thee I will all things endure.

OUR FATHER WHICH ART IN HEAVEN.

How sweet it is when o'er life's ocean driven,
  Tossed on the waves, or wrecked upon the shore,
To know we have a Father high in heaven,
  Who waits to lead us there when storms are o'er.
Storms cannot drive us from the love of God,
  Nor suffering, nor death, nor any pain,
And singing thus we bow beneath the rod,
  "Father in heaven, hallowed be thy name."

Hallowed be thy name for all thy care,
  For giving us thine own anointed Son,
To bear the burdens which we could not bear,
  To bleed and die for all that we have done.
What can we give Thee for that mighty love,
  Which caught us burning brands from out the flame?
We kneel in dust, and cry to thee above,
  "Father in heaven, hallowed be thy name."

When friends forsake us and the idols sweet,
　Are broken cisterns in the dark that we
Have reared, fall shattered at our feet,
　Whom look we, O our Father! but to thee?
Keep us, oh! keep us, 'neath thy shielding wing,
　For thou, O God! art ever more the same,
And teach us in each trying hour to sing,
　"Father in heaven, hallowed be thy name."

BE STILL, POOR HEART.

Be still, poor heart, though dim the way,
Beyond the darkness lies the day,
Beyond this tear-vale sweetly smiles
The sunlight of the Eden isles.

Be still, poor heart, if thou abide
Close to the Saviour's bleeding side,
No pang of grief that wrings the breast
Shall cloud the haven of thy rest.

Be still, poor heart, Gethsemane
Was trodden once for love of thee;
And Calvary's cross tells o'er each day
How Jesus bore thy sins away.

Be still, poor heart, and open now
To him who comes with thorn-crowned brow;
Drive out each soul-defiling sin,
And let the Lamb of God come in.

JESUS, TAKE ME HOME.

I AM growing weak and weary,
            Jesus, take me home.
Earthly scenes are dark and dreary,
            Jesus, take me home.
I long to see the heavenly plains,
Where everlasting beauty reigns,
And all that's best of life remains.

Home is dear, but heaven is dearer,
            Jesus, take me home.
Friends are near, but thou art nearer,
            Jesus, take me home.
That in a union sweet and close,
With life that never sorrow knows,
My wearied limbs may find repose.

Long my life has been declining,
            Jesus, take me home.
Pray I not with sad repining,
            Jesus, take me home.
Where faded youth revives again,
Without the teardrop or the pain,
The heavy cross and sinful stain.

Many friends have crossed the river,
            Jesus, take me home.
To their rest and thine forever,
            Jesus, take me home.
The nights and days pass slowly by,
While on my couch I wailing lie,
Waiting for Jesus, and to die.

When I've borne what is assigned me,
  Jesus, take me home.
When the test fire has refined me,
  Jesus, take me home.
My home, sweet home, I'm nearing fast,
The rough voyage o'er, its dangers past,
The harbor entering safe at last.

LOST JOY.

"Restore unto me the joy of thy salvation."

Oh! where is that delicious flood
 Of heavenly delight,
My soul enjoyed when Jesus' blood,
 First washed her garments white?

I miss the joy his name inspired,
 The rapture pure and sweet,
When sitting first in white attired,
 Before his wounded feet.

I know his love is never less
 Than infinitely deep,
And that sweet joy he gave to bless
 He wills that I should keep.

But I have wandered, Lord, from thee,
 And shunned to bear thy cross,
While joy and peace has fled from me,
 And mine has been the loss.

While low before thy feet I kneel,
    And my confessions pour,
Thy face in mercy, Lord, reveal;
    The joy I lost restore.

A SWEET CONFESSION.

"Lord, I have loved the habitation of thy house, and the place where thine honor dwelleth."

How sweet, when for a world that's new,
    Life's sun upon the old doth set,
To see the years pass in review,
    Without a fear or vain regret.

To know however much of care
    Has crossed the pathway newly trod,
That life has been a life of prayer,
    And faith upon the Son of God.

No place on earth has been so sweet,
    Nor habitation loved so well,
As that where saints together meet,
    And God himself delights to dwell.

Such hallowed memories cheer the way,
    That else were sad and full of gloom,
And light up with the glow of day
    The dreary entrance to the tomb.

How sweet in life's decline to know,
    That through our Lord's redeeming love,
We go from God's own house below,
    To that blest one prepared above.

SAFETY OF THE GOOD.

"The angel of the Lord encampeth round about them that fear him."

The good are safe, and need not fear
The danger distant seen, or near;
For at their side with flaming sword,
Doth walk the angel of the Lord.

With shield along the King's highway,
He safely keeps them through the day;
And where they spread their couch at night,
He watches till the morning light.

No fear may haunt, no foe molest,
Or shade of guilt disturb their rest;
When most opposed and sorest tried,
He points them to the Saviour's side.

Though pain shall waste them for the tomb,
That angel watches in the room,
And all things ready, leads the way
To portals of eternal day.

THE CHALLENGE OF A PURE HEART.

"Examine me, O Lord! and prove me."

O how great is that salvation,
   God hath sent from heaven above,
Bringing us in close relation
   To the Fountain of all love!

Vast that power, which, sin removing,
   Leaves the heart so full of trust,
That it calls God to the proving
   Of what once was sinful dust;

Seeks the process of refining,
   Where the great Refiner stays,
Till he sees before him shining
   The clear image of his face;

Asks for test that rudely dashes
   Every idol into dust,
That, like Job in fortune's ashes,
   It may prove its perfect trust.

PERFECT PEACE.

"Thou wilt keep him in perfect peace whose mind is stayed on Thee."

Oh, stay not the mind on the world and its pleasures,
   For restless and false every earthly delight;
At morn we repose on the strength of our treasures,
   And mourn they have left us ere cometh the night.

The peace that is perfect, serene and abiding,
   No pleasure of earth hath once promised or given;
'Tis found, all our hopes and our sorrows confiding
   In Jesus, and laying up treasure in heaven.

Our God is a rock, and the mind ever staying
　　On him, shall the peace of his being possess;
And tempests of sorrow his mandate obeying,
　　Disrobe all their terrors to brighten and bless.

My soul for this rest all the world hath forsaken;
　　Her wounds she would heal with its life-giving balm;
Oh, peace that is perfect, divine, and unshaken,
　　Encircle me now with thy sunlight and calm.

SECRET FAULTS.

"Cleanse Thou me from secret faults."

While before thy footstool kneeling,
　　All the loosened bonds set free,
Secret sins of thought and feeling
　　Looked upon alone by thee.

Save me from the wild heart beating
　　After pleasure while I pray,
And the guilt, like canker eating
　　All the better life away.

Save from sins in secret reigning,
　　Where thy love should but control,
And each secret folly staining
　　The white raiment of my soul.

Jesus by his word hath bidden
　　Me to sup with him and rest;
But the secret sins, though hidden,
　　Keep me ever from his breast.

While before thy footstool kneeling,
  Set me from the bondage free;
Secret sins of thought and feeling
  Looked upon alone by thee.

THE LORD'S SECRET.

"The secret of the Lord is with them that fear him."

Who shall understand the deep,
  Broad streams of life that round us flow?
Who shall that great secret keep,
  Which holy angels never know?

Who shall understand the ways
  Of God in form of flame or dove?
Tell how blend the mystic rays
  Of Justice and incarnate Love?

They who fear with holy fear,
  And with a blood-washed vision sweep
Things far distant and things near,
  The secrets of the Lord do keep.

When in prayer the lips unseal,
  Beneath the banner Christ unfurled,
God doth secret things reveal
  Withholden from the outer world.

To the lowly, pure in heart,
  Redeemed by blood from sinful curse,
God delighteth to impart
  The mysteries of his universe.

PLEASANT PLACES.

" The lines are fallen unto me in pleasant places."

A PLEASANT place is that where praise
   From holy hearts doth heavenward rise,
And mercy floods with golden rays
   The path of those who seek the skies.

And pleasant is that spot where flows
   The crimson tide that maketh clean,
And wearied soul in sweet repose
   On bosom of the Lord doth lean.

And pleasant that secluded place,
   Where faith with all prevailing might
Reveals the Saviour's loving face,
   And floods the soul with heavenly light.

They all are pleasant places where
   The heart is sanctified by grace;
And he whose very life is prayer
   Can always find a pleasant place.

THE TOUCH OF FAITH.

Hush! breathe not that I am coming; if he knew
    he might condemn;
But I feel my wound will vanish when I touch his
    garment's hem:
Great physicians have been spending all their
    skill upon my case,
But he bears a healing virtue in the sunshine of
    his face.

I have heard of wondrous healings he has wrought
    by word and touch,
And to speak my bleeding issue into soundness is
    not much;
Shall I raise a cry for mercy that will pierce his
    inmost soul?
No; if I can only touch him through the crowd,
    I shall be whole.

Oh the pressing of the people, just to see a sight
    pass by!
Give me room, room! I am dying for a cure he
    can supply;
Nearer, nearer, breathless, bleeding,—crush me
    not as I bow low!
Touched him! Oh what wondrous healing! and
    the Master will not know.

Shone her face with glory lighted, beat her heart
   for joy aloud;
Jesus turned upon her, speaking, "Some one
   touched me in the crowd."
Trembled all her soul within her as she bowed
   low in the dust,
Sobbing out the simple story of her sorrow and
   her trust.

Did the Great Physician spurn her, ask her pay
   for healing wrought?
Tell her she had rudely stolen what she should
   have humbly sought?
No; but his great heart of mercy yearned toward
   the trembling one,
While he whispered words of comfort, praising all
   that faith had done.

THE FATAL DELAY.

A MESSAGE had gone from the west to the east,
Inviting the world to sit down at the feast;
By highways and hedges, through back street and
   slum,
The King's servants went and compelled men to
   come.

There were many I-pray-thee-excuse-me's told,
For the love of a wife, farm, oxen, and gold;
The world won the rich, but the poor with delight
Went up to the banquet in garments of white.

But one had delayed — he was busy, no doubt;
Thought the King was too kind to let him stay
    out;
He often was warned, and would always reply,
A season convenient will come by and by.

Now, when the last moment had drifted away,
He saw the guests pass in their bridal array,
And heard from the banqueting-room far above
The triumph of song and the welcome of love.

Then the past came rebuking, spectre-like, grim;
Too late! Oh too late! there was no robe for him:
And a wail of despair went up to the skies,
Like that of the lost when he suddenly dies.

THE PRODIGAL SON.

RESTLESS.

Why should I be held in bondage, to a narrow
    world confined,
With the chains of sober plodding rusting through
    my heart and mind?
Shall the bird fill one ear only with the triumph
    of its song?
Or the eagle cease from soaring, when its wings
    are broad and strong?

Shall the river in its flowing out toward the
  boundless sea,
Stop in some low valley, saying, this is world
  enough for me?
Is a man born as a flower, but to wither where it
  blooms?
Is it crime to leave the shadow of the household
  gods and tombs?

Say, oh, balmy wind of summer! hailest thou not
  every land?
Speak, oh wild wave of the ocean! greetest thou
  not every strand?
Ho! ye winds and flowing rivers, ho! ye wingèd
  songsters, free;
God, who made you for my pleasure, made he not
  the *world* for me?

Sick am I, so sick and weary of this narrow,
  changeless clime,
Of the worn-out paths of custom, and the meas-
  ured steps of time;
Noble longings, born of manhood, meet delay in
  ceaseless strife,
Crumble into dust and ashes choking all the
  streams of life.

There's my brother, shallow-hearted, with whom
  things I hate agree,
Through his mean consent to being that which
  he should never be;
For the mind assumes the nature of the thing
  whereon it feeds,
And may narrow to the compass of the narrowest
  of creeds.

He had once a large ambition, but the sober
    world and skies
Wrought the blankness of his features and the
    deadness of his eyes;
He had hopes that dimmed the morning with the
    brightness of their glow,
But they settled down in shadows round his
    being long ago.

Now he loves what once he hated; and, his bat-
    tle banners furled,
Thinks his dreary round of doing all that makes
    the mighty world:
Let his soul rot out her splendor, let him quench
    her rising fires
In the deep and stagnant water of unsatisfied
    desires;

But I'll to the world's great highway, leaving nar-
    rower paths behind,
There to mingle with the fairest of all man and
    womankind;
Let the tendrils of affection in the glow of youth
    intwine
Round a nature that shall hold me to a larger
    soul than mine.

In my heart a pent up whirlwind storms and
    thunders at the door,
While the cry for life and freedom rings above it
    evermore;
Life, with ever changing sweetness, life, in all her
    rainbow hues,
Without rudeness of the Gentiles, without strait-
    ness of the Jews.

There is home! well, home is nothing, when it
    narrows down so small;
There are tender ties! what matter, when you
    have outgrown them all?
Home is where the heart reposes, and its love the
    strongest tie;
May be, down the golden future, I will just come
    home to die.

In the sylvan shades of pleasure, by her cool and
    placid streams,
I shall find the consummation of my brightest
    flood of dreams;
Let my brother scorn the venture, in the world I
    place my trust,
While he sits upon its threshold but to rotten and
    to rust.

Where's my portion, Father? Give it! be your
    silence doubt or scorn,
I should deem it weak to tarry in the place where
    I was born;
Thanks, farewell! the soothing murmur of the
    world's great undertone
Finds an answer in my bosom from a voice like
    to its own.

DRIFTING.

Ah, why did I stay so long
    Shut up in a cheerless night,
Away from the harp and song,
    Away from this world of light?

I drift on a sea of joy
　　To an ever joyous clime;
Why should the heart of a boy
　　Be withered before its time?

Drifting away from the cold,
　　Stiff form of a saintly hearth,
The new face buries the old
　　Down under its glow of mirth;
My father, he haunts me yet
　　With show of tears at the door;
My brother, I'll soon forget
　　What kind of a frown he wore.

Drifting away into life,
　　Be it right or be it wrong,
I love the glorious strife
　　Of this rosy land of song.
Drifting away from the pool
　　Of stagnant water and weeds,
Away from the iron rule
　　Of solemn faces and creeds.

THE FAR COUNTRY.

Here the birds have gayer plumage, floating under
　　bluer skies;
Here the flower is ever fragrant, and the summer
　　never dies;
Here is milk and honey flowing, wine and music,
　　dance and mirth;
Take me to thy heart of gladness, O thou paradise
　　of earth!

Here can dwell no narrow bigot, with a scripture
 quoting tongue,
Nor a priest cry from the altar at the sin of being
 young;
Here the living sorrow never, and the dying but
 deplore
They grew wearied out with pleasure when they
 might have tasted more.

Gone are all the solemn faces that did haunt me
 everywhere,
And the hollow, death-like moaning of that ever-
 lasting prayer.
What has youth to do with praying, singing slow
 and solemn psalms,
Sinking downward, vision-freighted, in the dead-
 est of all calms?

Come the moments overburdened with an ever
 varied bliss;
Was there ever life so golden, was there ever
 world like this?
Temples fling no dreary shadow, bells ring in no
 solemn fast;
'Tis enough to live the present without mourning
 for the past.

Pleasure, come, and drift me onward, thro' and
 thro' thy paradise,
With its sea of heaving bosoms, and its heaven of
 melting eyes!
Time is short to sip the nectar from each richly
 tinted flower,
Help me crowd a world of sweetness into every
 passing hour.

I will sound the depths of being, I will fathom
    all delights,
Till my soul dare not look backward lest she fal-
    ter in her flights;
I will scale the highest mountains, every binding
    chain destroy,
Till the fountains of my being break up into
    streams of joy.

Hear the pealing of the laughter! see the wine in
    rivers flow,
And the whirling of the dancers with their bosoms
    white as snow!
Hear the volume of the music like a mighty thun-
    der-roll,
Bidding all the merry-hearted to the banquet of
    the soul!

Now the joy-bells thrill their welcome; how their
    silver voices woo
From the old life, strait and narrow, to the
    other, broad and new!
Break thy bondage, heart, forever! plume thy
    pinions, soul of fire,
For the outer bound of pleasure, or in daring it
    expire.

SMITTEN.

Spectres, ghastly shadows wearing,
    Back to depths from whence ye rose!
Wild eyes, with your horrid staring,
    Will ye never, never close?

Heaven above, why art thou raining
　　Burning ashes through my brain?
Driving reason to her waning,
　　Never more to wax again?

What a night! did earth go reeling
　　Down with thunder-crash to hell?
For there comes a strange revealing
　　That somewhere a something fell
Shattered, with its fragments filling
　　All the waste its feet had crossed,
And the mighty heavens thrilling
　　With the fearful cry, "Lost! lost!"

DESTITUTION.

Destitute, cold, and alone,
　　With shame burnt into my brow,
And a face so altered grown
　　That nobody knows me now.
Old friends shrink out of my sight,
　　For the world is strangely made,
Giving a light for a light,
　　Giving a shade for a shade.

The gayest were round me drawn
　　When money a friend would buy,
But now that my portion's gone
　　They have left me here to die.
Of hell or of heaven above
　　This truth to my soul is born,
The deeper the world doth love,
　　The deeper the world doth scorn.

What though I have had my dream,
    And dregs are left in the cup,
The heart can itself redeem
    If it only will bear up.
Let hunger gnaw at my life,
    My very shadow be cursed,
I can dare the world to strife,
    And make the best of the worst.

Destitute, cold and alone,
    The glorious thing I did
Hath wrought me a bed of stone
    With rags for a coverlid.
I know far more than I knew,
    Though beaten and backward hurled:
I have seen all through and through
    The hollow heart of the world.

DEEPER DEPTHS.

How the hopes within me sicken,
    Feeding, for my bread, the swine!
All the land is famine stricken,
    Famine-smit, this soul of mine:
Perish — O my God! I perish!
    Deeper sink in misery!
Wonder if at home they cherish
    Any kindly thought for me?

Though I have spent all my living,
    Did my father know my pain,
Would he, now, the past forgiving,
    Take me to his home again?

Has my brother, shallow-hearted,
  Guiltless of my deep disgrace,
Ever languished since we parted
  To behold his brother's face?

Oh that I had never squandered
  Youth and fortune, honor, worth!
Oh that I had never wandered
  From the hallowed place of birth!
There was plenty round me waving,
  There all heart should wish was mine;
Now my hunger stirs a craving
  For the husky food of swine.

Comes the past around me stealing,
  Making loneliness more lone,
While a flood of tender feeling
  Melteth all my heart of stone.
I will home, though undeserving,
  Sorrow for the sinning done,
And ask but to die in serving
  Where I once was honored son.

HOMEWARD.

Frown thy worst, dark-splendid folly! mock my
  rags, ye passers by!
I will reach the home of boyhood, though I reach
  it but to die!
Home, still home, though left so madly; home,
  dear shelter, calm and sweet,
How I long to cross thy threshold, and to rest my
  weary feet!

Hollow-cheeked, and broken-hearted, with a load
    of rags and sin, —
O my brother! O my father! will ye know and
    let me in?
I will ask no seat of honor, but creep to the
    meanest place,
Where in serving I may hide me and my terrible
    disgrace.

I did dream the world so lovely, and its pleasures
    passing fair;
But beneath the gilded surface, oh the canker
    worm is there!
Better far the sober quiet of my father's saintly
    hearth,
Than the world's unhallowed laughter, and the
    whirlwind of its mirth.

Should my father spurn my pleading, and my
    brother vent his scorn,
I shall look upon their faces and the place where
    I was born:
Life would have a clearer setting, death would be
    a message sweet,
If I knew that I were dying somewhere near my
    father's feet.

Home, once mine, there, there I see it! spurned
    so madly, long ago!
Who comes running? not my father! one more
    bent and gray, I know.
Nearer, nearer, breathless, hasting; arms out-
    stretched and smiles I see!
O my father! O my father! love for me, even
    me?

Not the best robe — no, my father; not a jewel,
   not a ring!
Must I wear them? they will tarnish, worn by
   such a worthless thing.
Kill the fatted calf, my father! make a merry
   feast for one
So defiled, and all unworthy to be called again
   thy son!

Oh, what love! and oh what sorrow! I will never
   wander more;
Oh, what sadness and heart-breaking since we
   parted at this door!
Safe at home! how sweet the shadow, blest the
   calm that reigns around!
I was worse than dead, my father; I was lost —
   but now am found!

REST AMIDST UNREST.

"In the world ye shall have tribulation, but in Me ye shall have peace."

Storms without, but calm within,
   At peace, a world opposing;
Losing life a life to win,
   In strife, and yet reposing:
Hated when by love most blest,
   Friendless, and still befriended,
Restless, knowing perfect rest,
   Defenceless, yet defended.

Poor, and still possessing all,
    In tears rejoicing ever;
Light, where deepest shadows fall,
    Borne down, but fainting never;
Wanderers, yet not astray,
    Unblest, and ever blessing;
Tribulation all the way,
    But peace in Christ possessing.

SOUL BREATHINGS.

Come, thou Spirit, wounding, healing,
    In the form of flame or dove;
Come, with all thy great revealing
    Of a Saviour's dying love.

Waken every pure emotion,
    Scatter every rising fear,
That in deep and strong devotion
    To the cross we may draw near.

Come, the heaven of heavens unfolding,
    Crowns and kingdoms, shores of bliss,
That the future life beholding,
    We may lose our love of this.

Show us Jesus, bleeding, dying,
    While we sing; and as we pray,
His most precious blood applying,
    Wash our guilty stains away.

REST, REST!

Rest, rest, dear Lord, is there no place of rest,
 Where safe from storms my wearied soul may hide?
Nearer thy feet? with John, upon thy breast?
 Or far within the wound of thy dear side?

Rest, rest, dear Lord : my soul is tossed about, —
 Now anchored safe, now lost in stormy seas ;
Her passengers are anger, fear, and doubt,
 When they should be but love and joy and peace.

Rest, rest, dear Lord, oh hear my solemn cry,
 Surrounded where thou art with all the blest!
Didst thou not in whirlwinds of anguish die,
 That I might know thine own sweet after-rest?

Rest, rest, O Lord, send rest! the pain, the loss,
 Of this great strife is more than I can bear!
Nearer, I fainting press, unto thy cross ;
 O Lamb for sinners slain, receive me there!

IF 'TWERN'T FOR THE GRACE OF GOD.

If 'twern't for the grace of God I never had seen this day.
Six out of ten in the grave, and the others far away ;
Two are at work in the mines, one is afloat on the wave ;
The other, God only knows if in or out of the grave.

Two lying dead, and so white — they were boys,
　　in the early dawn, —
And the only girl that we had, in the next room,
　　almost gone;
Smoothing the hair of the boys, to hear her cry
　　" Home ! " and pass !
If 'twern't for the grace of God, I'd been down
　　under the grass.

One carried home in the night, the blood all over
　　his face ;
What should I do if I couldn't lean hard on the
　　blessed grace?
The other lingering, dying, sinking slowly away;
If 'twern't for the grace of God I never had seen
　　this day.

There's something about the grace, I don't under-
　　stand it quite,
That no matter what may come, it makes it ap-
　　pear all right ;
I've heard it often explained, in words that the
　　learned make,
But all I know, it's a thing that won't let my old
　　heart break.

GETHSEMANE.

The Saviour to the Garden strays,
　　The last sad supper o'er,
A burden on his spirit weighs,
And that sweet sadness of his face
　　Grows deeper than before.

GETHSEMANE.

    The loving John doth nearer press
      To soothe the Master's heart;
    So deep the pain of his distress
    He seeks the balm of loneliness
      In solitude apart.

Hush! through the stillness of the night,
A cry of weakness and of might
Breaks up the heavens, and onward rolls
Like waves of grief from wounded souls.
What is it? Hath some mighty wrong
Wrought discord in the angel song?
Doth heaven, from joy to sorrow grown,
With anguish shake the great White Throne?
Stars fall! worlds burn! is time no more?
Earth hath not heard such sounds before.
What is it? doth the death-wind break
The golden doors, and, smiting, take
The crown of life from him who wears
Lightly eternal years, and bears
The universe as though its weight
Were but a shadow, and not great?
See! far above night-shadows, dim,
The cherubim and seraphim,
With countless angels, breathless gaze
Upon that spot where Jesus prays
"My Father!" and the mountains nigh
Refuse to echo such a cry!
While through the universe there runs
A shudder, smiting outer suns.
"My Father!" and the starry train
Stands in the darkness struck with pain,
And whitens every face above
To hear the moan of bruised love.

Spread, spread thy wings, dark-plumèd night,
And hide that scene from mortal sight.
"O Father! Father! if it be
But possible to love and thee,
Take now this bitter cup from me!"
A silence deep, unearthly, dread,
As though the universe were dead.
No song in heaven, — on earth no sound,
The Saviour prostrate on the ground,
And near him, through that sorrow deep,
The three disciples, fast asleep.
O what a dark, dread, solemn hour!
What flows of grief, what throes of power!
When human weakness drops the cup,
Then strength divine doth take it up:
Now cross and pain the victory wins.
Then a lost world's forgiven sins:
Now hell breaks on his weeping eyes,
And now white robes in Paradise;
While far above that dreadful spot
The Father hears, but answers not.
No answer? See! from yonder height
An angel comes with rapid flight.
Oh hath the Father changed his plan
Of asking blood to ransom man?
Comes this strong angel from the sky
To tell the Lord he need not die?
Say, spirit bright, what tidings now?
He heeds not — fanning Jesus' brow.
Oh tell us, what of that dread cup?
He heeds not — holding Jesus up.
Say, what of hope dost thou impart?
Behold! he binds the Saviour's heart,

And vanishes through shadows dim,—
He only came to strengthen him.
Hope? some hope far off unfolds!
With firmer grasp the Saviour holds
The bitter cup; the grief he bore
Flies, while a joy set on before
Doth fill the darkness now with light,

Doth change his weakness into might;
The cross grows sweet, and sweet the pain,
And sweeter still the after gain;
The agony to rapture turns,
And love with tenfold glory burns!
A sob, a sigh, the battle's won —
"Father! thy will, not mine, be done!"

THY WILL, NOT MINE.

There is no life on earth, though calm and bright it be,
But has a sorrow-spot, some dark Gethsemane;
Where in fierce fires of pain, strong cries and blinding tears,
The God who loves us best, as loving not appears.

Thrice happy is that heart, which, bruised, on God doth fall,
Feeling 'tis answered best when answered not at all;
And wrestling with his will shall find the battle won
By that deep cry of trust — thy will, not mine, be done.

Our feeble wills lay hold on light and quiet rest,
When pain and tears would make us what God
    loves the best;
And they, who, full of trust, earth's weight of
    sorrow bear,
Shall evermore in heaven a cloudless sunshine wear.

We walk through darkness here that we may
    reach the light;
We fall in weakness now that we may rise in might;
And when to that high will we bow, and cease
    from strife,
The hallowed peace of God encircles all our life.

THE RIVER OF LIFE.

"I saw a pure river of water of life."

Here, where the life behind and the life before
    doth meet,
A river of crystal cool, where pilgrims lave their
    feet;
I step from its shade of palm; touching the gentle wave,
I lose the smell of the mould, brought up out of
    the grave.

Fled is the fever and dust of earth's ignoble strife;
Dawning with sweet surprise the visions of life
    on life;
While at the river's touch there cometh with slow
    increase,
Infinite sweep of thought and fathomless depth
    of peace.

Roll on, sweet river of life, and change me
    through and through,
Till all that was old and worn be wrought into
    the new ;
Wash out old narrowing creeds, giving the golden
    link
Of that great chain of thought the loftier angels
    think.

Gone is the aged heart, and changed is the weary
    brain ;
Cometh the youth that I lost more youthful back
    again ;
Oh wash me, river of bliss, until from lip and eye
Flashes the fire of a life that never more can die.

MARY MAGDALENE.

In the darkness God had met her,
  Gave her sorrow for the wrong
Of a heart bound by the fetter
  Of a sin seven devils strong.
Through the gossip of the city,
  And a voice that spake within,
She found one who would have pity
  On a fallen child of sin.

Through the sweet pain from love's quiver
  Cried she, weeping o'er the past,
" What gift shall I bring the Giver
  Of all gifts for love so vast?

I will purchase precious ointment,
   Seeking me worn is my Lord;
While I soothe him with anointment,
   He may soothe me with his word."

Pharisee sat rudely staring
   With the blankness of surprise;
Jesus, heavenly welcomes wearing,
   Shone forgiveness from his eyes;
The new life came o'er her sweeping,
   Broke her heart, and kneeling there,
She did wash his feet by weeping,
   And did wipe them with her hair.

While the Pharisee sat frowning,
   Others o'er the gift made strife,
Jesus sat, her Saviour, crowning
   Mary with an endless life.
Could a box of ointment borrow
   Smile from Jesus half so sweet?
No; it was that flood of sorrow
   As she kissed the Saviour's feet.

SORROW AND JOY.

"Weeping may endure for a night, but joy cometh in the morning."

Our sorrows come as comes the night,
To vanish in the morning light;
And tears we shed in doubt and fear,
Like dews in sunshine disappear.

Though long the night, and sad our way,
The joy will dawn with dawning day;
And darkest hour of grief is born
Beneath the purple ridge of morn.

Though sad we part from those we love,
With joy we meet them all above.
And things that wear a shadow here,
In heaven with joyous light appear.

What shadow deep and sullen gloom
Broods o'er the silence of the tomb!
Yet from its bosom, for the skies,
A joyous world shall singing rise.

REMEMBER ME.

Lord, amidst thy pain and grief,
Canst thou love a dying thief?
Though the thorns press on thy brow,
Wilt thou turn and bless me now?
Look I from myself to thee,
Dying Lord, remember me.

All my guilt I need not tell,
For thou knowest it full well;
And in death I feel thou art
All I need to cleanse my heart;
To thy wounds for help I flee,
Dying Lord, remember me.

Can it be my plea prevails?
From the thorns and from the nails
Leaps the blood, and seems to fall
O'er my black heart, cleansing all;
Thou dost sweetly own that plea,—
Dying Lord, remember me.

What, my Lord, to day with thee
In paradise, where angels be?
Though it seems so vast, my Lord,
Never will I doubt thy word;
Thy great kingdom I shall see,
For thou hast remembered me.

THE WONDROUS ON BEFORE.

Flash the moments by like quivers
　　Shot from Time's unerring bow,
And the years like swollen rivers
　　Crush their way with ceaseless flow;
Sun and moon, bright constellations,
　　Seas of glory without shore,
All that are and once were nations,
　　Near the wondrous on before.

We have seen its glory streaming
　　O'er the sky and hallowed page;
And through all the poet's dreaming
　　Drifts the music of an age
When the wrong things shall be righted,
　　Justice rule for evermore,
Where all darkness shall be lighted
　　In the wondrous on before.

It is coming, coming nearer,
   With its shadowings sublime;
It is dawning, dawning clearer,
   O'er the wrinkled brow of time;
Age of glory, age of wonder,
   Wrought to reign for evermore,
Breaketh now with crash of thunder
   From the wondrous on before.

THE DESIRED HAVEN.

"Then are they glad, because they be quiet; so he bringeth them to their desired haven."

Quiet, quiet, glad are they,
   Anchored by the peaceful shore;
Glad to end a rock-bound way,
   Quiet, for the storms are o'er.

This the haven long desired,
   So the Lord hath safely brought
His beloved, worn and tired,
   To the heavenly rest they sought.

Glad, because the deathless life
   Lightens all things with its glow;
Quiet, for the sea of strife
   Ceased to follow long ago.

Sad and restless they set sail
   On the waste of stormy seas;
Quiet, glad, within the vail,
   Anchor they in perfect peace.

SABBATH EVE.

Go not yet, O sabbath eve!
  Calm and holy and serene;
Tarry still, nor take thy leave,
  For how happy we have been!
We have sung sweet songs of love,
  We have seen the Saviour's face,
While the Spirit, like a dove,
  Spread his wings o'er all the place:
Stay a while, nor leave us so,
Blessings still on all bestow.

And it seems as here we sit,
  'Tween the shadow and the light,
Holy angels round us flit,
  Prompting thought to heavenward flight;
Fled are all the ills of life,
  Gone the shadow and the grief,
And this quiet in the strife
  Seems most beautiful, though brief:
Eve of song, of praise and prayer,
Tarry yet, thou art so fair!

Drinking deep of holy things,
  Spirits linger, thirsting still,
Upward borne on mighty wings,
  Soar they unto Zion's hill,
Where the Son of Man bowed down
  'Neath a world's great load of sin,
Winning for our souls a crown,
  And a heaven to enter in:
Sabbath eve! O hour of bliss!
Stay, we love to think of this.

There's an eve to every day,
　There's a night to every noon,
And the thing we wish to stay
　Seemeth but to fly more soon;
And this sabbath eve so sweet
　Hasteth on before the night;
As we part so may we meet,
　In the endless sabbath light.
Eve of glory, richly wrought,
Go, but leave all thou hast brought.

EVEN SO, COME, LORD JESUS!

Jesus, once for sinners slain,
We are waiting for thy reign;
All the Church in raiment white
Stand prepared by day and night,
With the cry of lips now dumb,
Even so, Lord Jesus, come!

Though we never saw thy face,
Yet, partakers of thy grace,
We have loved thee though unseen;
Now, without a cloud between,
We would on thy glory gaze,
And behold thee face to face.

Come, Lord Jesus! through the sky
Let the herald angel fly!
Come, Lord Jesus! let thy tread
Fire the stars, and wake the dead!
Come, thou long-expected King,
We would meet thee while we sing.

THE BIRTHPLACE OF A SOUL.

"The Lord shall count when he writeth up the people, that this man was born there."

Our God shall say, when he doth count
　The mighty, bloodwashed scroll,
Upon this prayer-devoted mount
　Was born a precious soul.

Here wrestled men of mighty faith
　With Christ, in loving strife,
Until a soul from endless death
　Was born to endless life.

O hallowed spot, what memories sweet,
　Beholding thee, arise!
For here a soul did Jesus meet
　And win it for the skies.

Engrave the scenes of blood and strife
　On fame's decaying scroll,
But write upon the Book of Life
　The birthplace of a soul.

THE POWER OF FAITH.

"By faith the walls of Jericho fell down."

When they heard the trumpets blow
Round the walls of Jericho,
Gave they back a shout of scorn
To the blast of every horn.
　　This the way
　　Truth fares to-day.

Still the trumpets louder blew,
And the scorning fiercer grew,
While that strange, discordant band
Onward marched at God's command:
    This the way
    Truth works to-day.

Seven times round the walls they went,
Seven times back the scorn was sent;
Midst the horn-blast and the yell,
Jericho in ruins fell:
    This the way
    Truth works some day.

THE YOUNG RULER.

Sorrowful and broken-hearted
  Turned the ruler to his gain;
Jesus for the cross departed,
Gold his loving purpose thwarted,
  And they never met again.
Never will meet till the parted
  Heavens burning worlds shall rain.

Oh that gold should be so blinding,
  By the nearness of its shine!
Oh that gold should be so binding,
With its gilded circles winding
  Round a heart with serpent-twine,
That was beating to the finding
  Of all that is most divine!

Jesus loved him, as he, kneeling,
    Asked the gift of priceless worth,
Saw the light of holy feeling
O'er his spirit gently stealing,
    In the dawn of heavenly birth,
But the gold-dust sent him reeling
    Back again to lowest earth.

Jesus loved him for the using
    All the light he had to use,
And unfolded for his choosing
That which he at once refusing,
    Nothing higher could refuse;
So for fear of something losing
    Lost all that is loss to lose.

This is how God conquers evil,
    Asking things we love the best:
Joseph fled a guilty revel,
Job in ashes fought the Devil,
    Abram stood the crushing test:
Jesus only sought to level
    The young ruler's path to rest.

Well he knew his gold would beat him
    Backward every step, and sad,
Knew the tempting fiend would meet him
And with subtle lurings cheat him
    Out of all that maketh glad:
The one way he could defeat him
    Was to sell out all he had.

THE GUIDE AND GOAL.

"Guide me with thy counsel, and afterward receive me to glory."

Thy glory, Lord, I wish to reach,
   Glory of life, glory of thought;
By thine unerring counsel teach,
   And I shall be divinely taught.

I seek a glory known in part,
   Glory of Christ's eternal reign;
Beat from thy bondage, yearning heart,
   That losing all things this thou gain.

I seek a glory deep and calm,
   Beyond the blue, star-fleeted sea,
Where every thought doth fill with psalm
   The breathings of eternity.

Oh glory of the perfect man,
   Reposing in the perfect God,
And learning how the ages ran
   Before a weary world was trod!

Oh glory to be lifted high
   Above this realm of aimless strife!
Oh glory, never more to die,
   But drifting on from life to life!

The glory of all glorious things,
   And by a higher glory crowned,
Where spreads the majesty of wings,
   To fold a universe around.

I near the best of all that's best,
  Where awe itself is overawed,
And perfect forms in thoughtful rest
  Lean on the mysteries of God.

Lest from the path I turn aside,
  O Holy Spirit, sweetly teach!
Thy counsels ever be my guide,
  Till I the goal of glory reach.

STONE TROUBLES.

"Who will roll us away the stone?"

When through long and faithless praying
  All our hopes have withered grown,
We pause in our duty, saying,
  Who will roll away the stone?

When we seek to find out Jesus,
  And the light of perfect day,
Clinging to the things that please us
  Is the great stone in our way.

Ever sowing, never reaping,
  In the Master's field, alone,
Doubt will ask, while Faith is sleeping,
  Who will roll away the stone?

Stones of doubt keep back the blessing
  God is waiting to impart;
Stones of fear stop the confessing
  Which would ease a burdened heart.

Light and life would dawn the faster
  O'er the vale of whitened bones,
If the people and the pastor
  Would let God roll back the stones.

WAITING AT THE POOL.

Thousands stand to-day in sorrow,
        Waiting at the pool,
Saying they will wash to-morrow,
        Waiting at the pool;
Others step in left and right,
Wash their stained robes pure white,
Leaving you in sorrow's night,
        Waiting at the pool.

Souls, your filthy garments wearing,
        Waiting at the pool,
Hearts, your heavy burdens bearing,
        Waiting at the pool,
Can it be you never heard
Jesus long ago hath stirred
The waters with his mighty word,
        Waiting at the pool?

Thousands once were standing near you,
        Waiting at the pool,
Come their voices back to cheer you,
        Waiting at the pool;
Back from Canaan's happy shore,
Sorrow past and labor o'er,
Where they stand in tears no more,
        Waiting at the pool.

Mother leaves the son, the daughter,
          Waiting at the pool,
Calls to them across the water,
          Waiting at the pool;
You can never more embrace
Mother, or behold her face,
If you keep the leper's place,
          Waiting at the pool.

Step in boldly — death may smite you,
          Waiting at the pool;
Jesus may no more invite you,
          Waiting at the pool;
Faith is near you, take her hand,
Seek with her the better land,
And no longer doubting stand
          Waiting at the pool.

I PASSED DOWN THE VALLEY THEY SAY IS SO LONE.

I PASSED down the valley they say is so lone,
   It was crowded with pilgrim-feet,
On their way to the rule of a love-built throne,
   Where the good and the holy meet.

There was not a shadow to darken the way,
   For shadow there never can be,
Where the soft, sweet light of a heavenly day
   Breaks out from the throne and the sea

Of glass, like to crystal, where harpers thrill,
  With an ever-varying strain,
The soul with the music of God's great will,
  That death should be glorious gain.

I had dreamed in the world that lieth behind,
  Of struggles with death in the gloom,
But living we doubt, and in dying we find
  No path is so bright as the tomb.

DAVID'S CURE FOR A FAINT HEART.

"I had fainted unless I had believed to see the goodness of the Lord
in the land of the living."

ALL along life's weary road,
Hearts are breaking 'neath their load,
Strong men faint and ask to die,
When God's angel passes by,
Smiting here and smiting there,
All that's beautiful and fair.

Minds deep versed in nature's laws
Faint when God his smile withdraws;
They who doubt, with boastings loud,
Pallid grow before the shroud,
While beneath death's flag unfurled
Faint and sicken half the world.

He alone whose faith is firm
That beyond the shroud and worm
God's great goodness will appear,
Never comprehended here,
He alone, though sad his lot,
Bears a heart that fainteth not.

CONSOLATION IN CHRIST.

O hearts, forever aching to sink
    Down into the silence, and ache no more!
O brains, whose wearisome think, think, think,
    Make mystery darker than 'twas before!
Sweet rest in Jesus the weary find,
And heavenly light each darkened mind.

O eyes that long to be closed and hid
    Away from the burning heat of brain,
Under the shade of a coffin-lid,
    Never to burst into life again,
Looking on Jesus there doth arise
The mellowed glories of Paradise!

O hands that are weary winning bread,
    And feet that bleed on a thorny way,
Fearing the shadow of darkness fled,
    Fearing the light of a coming day,
Jesus hath purchased a refuge sweet
By his wounded hands and wounded feet!

LIGHT AT EVENTIDE.

When the lips "good-by" shall quiver,
    To the world and all beside,
Light shall come across the river,
    Just about the eventide;
It will be when moons are waning,
    Through a long night, dim with dews,
Light will flood the darkness, staining
    All my soul with heavenly hues.

Suddenly, in swift transition,
　　Life will leap from blinded clay,
To the full and open vision
　　Of a bright and cloudless day;
It will be when tears are gushing
　　At the coldness of the tide,
That this strange light will come rushing,
　　Just about the eventide.

Soul will look out from her prison,
　　Darkened long by doubt and sin,
To behold a new sun risen,
　　And the angels looking in;
See the doors, as Paul and Silas
　　Saw them open swift and wide;
This will be when dreams beguile us,
　　Just about the eventide.

Deathless friends, whom death did sever,
　　Building graves to baffle them,
Met at last, shall walk together
　　In the new Jerusalem;
Things that would not show their rightness,
　　Wherefores sought, but long denied,
Will shine out with wondrous brightness
　　In that light at eventide.

All the false outside and fashion
　　Of this world shall pass away,
And the self-crowned king of passion
　　Shall resign his blighting sway;
Contradictions of our being,
　　Questions none could e'er decide,
Will be settled and agreeing
　　In that light at eventide.

IN THE STRANGE DARKNESS.

In the strange darkness which the stars peer thro',
   'Mid the wild flowers that know not why they spring,
A song came drifting downward with the dew,
   Such as the angels and the children sing.

It had no rhyme or measure in its flow,
   But, oh! it made me bow, and weep, and kneel;
'Twas made beyond the range of stars; I know
   Humanity could not so sing and feel.

My friend, who walked beside me, heard no strain,
   And wondered why I wept who had no care;
He said that there was music in my brain,
   When there was something singing in the air.

I heard the melody of deep things yet
   To be unfolded, friend, to me and you,
And saw the light of suns that never set,
   On heaven's horizon, through the falling dew.

CHRIST NEEDS A WORKING CHURCH.

Go into the streets and lanes,
   Tell the gospel news:
Too much working power remains
   Sitting in the pews.
Satan works outside the fold,
   We must meet him there;
Wrest the captives from his hold,
   Break their chains by prayer.

CHRIST NEEDS A WORKING CHURCH.

Go into the haunts of crime
  With a hero's heart;
Tell of Jesus' love sublime,
  Till the warm tears start.
Tell the harlot Christ forgave
  Mary all her sin;
Tell the drunkard Christ can save,
  And heaven let him in.

Men are wanted who will praise
  God in back-street mire
Like they do on Sabbath days,
  Sitting in the choir.
Easy work to sing and pray
  In the cushioned seat;
Do it on the broad highway,
  In the crowded street.

Women wanted who will nurse,
  Praying with the sick,
Where lips utter fearful curse
  Every time they speak;
Thousands such God greatly needs,
  Ay, and thousands more,
Who will teach Christ, not their creeds,
  To the sinful poor.

Far into the deep launch out,
  Sink the heavy dredge,
There are but few fish about
  Near the water's edge.
Let those hold the endmost ropes
  On the even beach,
Whose weak faith and dying hopes
  Cannot farther reach.

INCOMPREHENSIBLE WEALTH.

"God, who is rich in mercy."

To be rich is to possess
More of blessing than can bless,
Having all our wants supplied
And abundant wealth beside.
Who the love of God can know
When his mercy doth o'erflow?

Rich in mercy! He whose might
Built the worlds, and gave them light!
Rich in mercy! Can it be?
There is mercy, then, for me.
None so lost as need despair,
If a God such riches bear.

Come who need, and come who will,
God is rich in mercy still.
Wealth so vast could not exhaust
Though ten thousand worlds were lost.
If a universe should fall,
Love so great could cover all.

Rich in mercy! be it sung
In every land, by every tongue;
Rich in mercy! let the cry
To the distant nations fly!
Come who need, and come who will,
God is rich in mercy still.

THE GLORIOUS DECLARATION.

"The heavens declare the glory of God."

Oh! not by chance, or strength of time,
Arose the universe sublime,
Nor by a self-creative might
Revolve the planets, trailing light.
I hear them cry, sun, moon, and star,
"Our God did make us what we are."

From age to age, in lines of fire,
They write the glory of their Sire;
Unworn by time or length of days,
They hymn their great Creator's praise,
Nor ever voice or sound has stirred
The bounds their language has not heard.

Forth from his blue, star-curtained bed,
The sun doth as a bridegroom tread,
And viewing all the boundless space,
Rejoices to begin his race,
Diffusing light and heat from God,
O'er paths by men and angels trod.

Oh! tell it sun, and tell it moon,
In calm of night, and glare of noon;
Oh! tell it star, and planet bright,
Tell it myriad worlds of light,
From age to age the truth rehearse,
That God did build the universe.

A GREAT DEEP.

"Thy judgments are a great deep."

How strange thy judgments are, O God,
    Thy majesty how dread!
The nations fall beneath thy rod,
    The streets are filled with dead.

The pestilence at thy command
    Doth through our cities sweep;
Thy judgments none can understand,
    A great and awful deep.

Our pride and hopes lie shattered now,
    And things we thought secure;
Eternity, O God! and thou
    Alone unscathed endure.

Before the fathomless abyss
    Of judgment though we weep,
We know the depth of mercy is
    Far deeper than that deep.

Though flame-blast swept the worlds above,
    And time itself were done,
We rest securely in thy love,
    For Jesus is thy Son.

NEAR GOD.

It has been the one wish of all my life,
　That when Death lays on me his heavy rod,
And I have borne my share of this world's strife,
　I may wake up and find myself near God.

Not far away, in darkness and alone,
　Or midst huge shadows undefined and dim,
But near the glorious circle round his throne,
　That I may hear the angels chant their hymn.

And see around me, ay, close at my side,
　Dear lost ones, loving, beautiful and true,
Basking in sunshine this world had denied,
　Where never shadow comes or evening dew.

Then care will never cloud, or make me seem
　Less noble than God wills my soul should be,
And I shall realize my brightest dream,
　Of chainless thought and immortality.

The wish may seem presumptuous, but I dread
　To be shut out from light, as night from day,
To be a living soul, yet seeming dead,
　Where death itself stands evermore at bay.

WAITING FOR THE ANGEL.

Shut the house up as forsaken,
　Put the lights out in the hall,
I would sleep, and never waken
　Till I hear the angel call.

Every morn for seeming ages,
    Life's great book I've opened wide,
Pondered o'er its mystic pages
    Till they grew more mystified.

I will wait until there lighten
    From within and from without,
New revealings that shall brighten
    Into clearness every doubt.
I would sleep, nor care to waken,
    Till the Lord shall waken all,
Till the very earth be shaken,
    And I hear the angel call.

Then will come the perfect showing
    Of things distant and things near,
And unto the fuller knowing
    Will the greater God appear.
Therefore bar the window tightly,
    Put the lights out in the hall,
I would sleep serene and lightly
    Till I hear the angel call.

GOD KNOWS.

Men know not the earnest praying
    That ascends from vale and town,
For a lost world, ever weighing
    All the good and holy down.
God knows, for the mighty pleading,
    Whitens half the judgment scroll,
And the Lamb, once faint and bleeding,
    Sees the travail of his soul.

Men know not why lips so sainted
  Faltered out " Good-by " so soon ;
Why the great heart, stricken, fainted
  In the foremost ranks at noon.
God knows ; it may be to teach us
  That against permitted odds,
In a day that may not reach us,
  God will triumph o'er all gods.

Men know not why to the dwelling
  Where they pray both morn and night,
Sin comes, like the simoom, felling
  Youth and beauty with its blight.
God knows ; he may see hearts squander
  Love, and Christ unheeded knock.
Better lambs a while should wander,
  Than to ruin all the flock.

Men know not why Christ, our Master,
  Comes not back to earth again ;
Why his kingdom spreads no faster,
  In a world where he must reign.
God knows ; and I fear the showing
  Of the judgment day will be,
They who did the gospel sowing,
  Did not sow on bended knee.

God knows how much faith we mingle
  In each hand of scattered grain ;
If we labor with eye single
  To his glory, or for gain.
God knows every secret feeling,
  Why we sing and why we weep ;
In that day of great revealing,
  God knows what we all shall reap.

MAN IMPEACHED BY NATURE.

I DREAMED, and lo, a voice did thunder loud
Down through the universe, and echo called
To echo with shrill, ghostlike cry, until
Calm Silence fled amazed, and hid herself
In a dim waste beyond the rolling worlds.
Then gathered round a great white throne in
    heaven,
Bright spirits, crowned with the strong youth of
    countless
Years, on whose unwrinkled brows the radiance
Of God's smile flowed lightly ever;
And man, all bowed and broken, there stood out
Before God and the angels, charged with crime.

Then Nature spake: Almighty Father, God,
Eternal, just, and only wise, supreme,
Who makest all things for a glorious end,
And hatest wrong, thou didst create me pure,
And call me to thy ministry of love,
Pronouncing with the sweet approval of
Thy voice, my form most perfect, my mission
Most divine. Then did these high arches ring
With grateful song from bird, stream, river, the
Swaying forests, and the far-sweeping seas.
And I was glad, my Father, at thy feet
To wait and minister, in garments pure,
To man, a noble being, whom thou didst
Command to rise from out my dust and be,
Crowning him with the fire of thine own life.
Nor have I once withholden from him aught

Of that vast wealth thou gav'st me for his sake.
The breezes fanned his brow, the light and shade
Wove varied splendor at his feet. He walked
On flowers through Edens of delight, and breathed
The incense from my altars ere it rose
To thee. His life was one long pause of joy.
I wore no scar from wrathful bolt, nor was
My bosom rent with rude volcanic shock,
But everywhere from out my rounded form,
Pregnant with beauty, flashed a new glory,
Steeping his senses in perpetual bliss.
Ye priests and kings in this unfading clime,
Where suns set not, and moons can never wane,
He, against whom I enter solemn plea,
Was compassed round with that strong arm of
    love
On which you lean; your joys were his, your
    peace,
Eternal, fathomless, serene, unmoved
By storm of sighs, or flood of bitter tears,
Touched, and becalmed with blessedness, his life.
And that same smile which brightens all your
    brows,
Fell, like a benediction, round his heart,
Thrilling it through with hopes that make new
    heavens
Break out above the old with crowns of life.
And never melody rolled from my harp,
And never song gushed from my warbling choirs,
Nor herb or flower sprang from my breast, that did
Not tell him of my Maker and his own.
O sons of light and joy! was he not blest,
Raised by the power of a sweet restraint

To that high place, where, choosing good for its
Own sake, he could prove worthy of his trust,
And crown his soul with never ending bliss?

Didst thou not also come, O Judge, supreme!
And converse hold with him at eventide,
When the long shadows lay across the world,
And o'er the western wave a bridge was wrought
Of molten gold, that stretched from heaven to
 earth?
Thy voice I heard with solemn awe; so great
It was that echo feared to speak it back.
Thy tread, and all the light of thy vast form,
Moving in majesty about my heart,
Gave birth to hopes crowned with eternal bloom.
O sons of light and joy! I fondly dreamed
That summer upon summer, through all time,
Would deck my brow with ever bright'ning flow-
 ers,
And never desolating wind break out,
Smiting with death the child of grace and song.

Alas, how fallen have I been! my breast,
Made but to throb with life, hath borne the dead
For ages, — dead man, dead brute, dead flower,
 bird,
Leaf. Palsy hath smit my limbs, rottenness,
And hideous forms of slow decay, hath set
Their teeth into my vitals, and the grave
Hath been my bosom friend, the skull, the worm,
My ever-present guests, unbidden, loathed,
Thrust on me by the sin of him who stands
At heaven's high bar, before the Judge of all.

Hear me, ye wise and pure! In one short hour,
Oh, what a wreck was wrought! Hushed the glad
   song,
And crushed the flowers that plumed a thousand
   hills.
Immortality, struck through with mortal
Pangs, looked out on death and died. Red ruin
Struck his heel into my heart; the canker
And the blight did slay and eat the blossom;
While that which was a paradise of life
Became a tomb, where death sat on his spoils.
Should you pure river flowing from the throne
Be turned to blood, the sapphire walls around
You crumble to decay, the cherubim
And seraphim, with flaming wings fall down;
The tree of life be withered, and the bells
Which ring long sabbaths in, knell for the dead
Borne through the golden streets, what grief were
   yours?
Such grief was mine. I pray you hear my plea.

Would not a soul from which all goodness had
Not fled, beholding what its sin had wrought,
Bow down in grief, and by repentant tears
Seek to repair the waste, bring back the bloom,
The light, the song, and so crush out its guilt?
Stands there a record on that book, which holds
The thoughts and deeds of man in every age,
Of tears once shed, or sighs once heaved? Did
   he
Not measure out the narrow span to which
He brought his life, by deeds more foul, till heaven
From off my bosom wiped the last faint trace

Of human feet, and we came forth baptized
Into what should have been a nobler life?

Fair forms and pure, again rose at his feet,
The heavens were arched with rainbow hues,
    through which
God smiled a promise of unfading love;
Sweet children, dowered with rare gifts and grace,
Like unto those which blest my early life,
Came with the light of long-forgotten joys,
And though they needs must die in the full bloom,
'Twas but to live again in lovelier forms.
Was there not also thrown about man's heart
Some holy influence from this peaceful clime,
The shadow of an awful form of love,
Which strove by gentle argument to win
Him back to all and more than he had lost?
One moment did he pause and upward gaze,
But lest the better life should reign, brake loose,
And, leagued with him who waged fierce war in
    heaven,
Out-demoned all his former self, and made
Me but a scroll whereon to write his crimes.

Did I not bring him blessings? But he wrought
Them into that which cursed all people, and
Through the mighty realms of thought spread
    death, forged
Chains, broke hearts, and set the vacant stare of
Madness into calm eyes, from which pure souls
Beamed forth, till the wild frenzy, born of wine,
Steeped all their glory in a dread eclipse.
Wherefore, all solemnly I urge my plea,

In this high court, as one who suffers wrong.
I call on seas, the dead which in them lie,
The wrecks which crowd their strands; I call on
    rocks,
Hills, caverns, mountains, whole armies buried
Under fair smiling plains, ruined cities,
Dread implements of war wrought from my wealth,
The sword, blood-stained thrones, Fame's blazing
    scroll,
And sepulchres o'er which torn banners wave,—
On these I call to witness that proud man,
To work ignoble ends, hath turned my good
To ill, my sweet to bitter, and my light
To dark, heaping upon me endless shame.

Anon he worshipped me, pronounced me God,
The cause, the centre, and the sum of all
That is; eternal, self-existent; and
From out my dust, reared temples unto dust,
The masonry of tombs, the crown of death.
But ever did I beat his worship back
With the sad homily of falling leaves,
And point him up to that which never dies.
Gold he did worship, built his hopes on that;
Wood, the unthinking herd, the shapeless stone,
And loathsome things that crawl through slime
    to die.
Sun, moon, and stars, all ghostly shapes, foul
    forms,
He clothed with attributes they never wore,
Blaspheming that pure name which hallows all.
Oh, 'twas pitiful, to see a deathless
Soul lay hold on dying things, grasp shadows,

And to unfathomable deeps launch out,
With chart nor helm that strove for shores of rest.

Behold him now ; how fallen doth he seem !
And yet I pray you, ere ye weep his fate,
Look on my wasted form, fresh from the fire,
The fearful burnings of the last great day
Of time, wherein the heavens did melt and flow
In one vast sea of flame, dissolving all
That congregation of fair forms which clung
Around my breast, strewing with ghastly wrecks,
Torn worlds, rent systems, the eternal shores
Hear me, I pray ; the pure alone are just.

Then through my dream, I saw stern Justice rise,
In wrathful form, with a huge sword to smite ;
But Mercy, clad in sunshine, stood between
The sword and man ; while in their midst a cross
Of gold uprose, shining these words on all :
Behold, I make new heavens and new earth,
Wherein pure righteousness shall reign, and all
The former things shall pass away, — the tears,
The sorrow and the pain — and death shall die.

Then 'neath that cross down at God's feet they bowed
In blissful reconcilement, and clasped hands.
So passed my dream, as sabbath morning dawned.

THE DEATH OF TIME.

The verdict had gone forth, and Death, with axe
Of flame, amidst a wreck of human skulls,
Crowns, thrones, stood waiting by the block for
 Time;
While he, as one who takes farewell of love,
And feels it harder than to die, lingered.
Through halls of state and gorgeous palaces
A doomèd king he walked where once he reigned.
The chiselled wonders of his fitful rule;
Science and art still in the glow of youth;
The pen, the harp, the sword: all lovely forms
Of life that he had loved, met the last gaze
Of eyes too kingly for the balm of tears.
He kissed the flowers and bade them weep no
 more;
He laid his hand on seas and hushed their moan;
The sob of brooks and streams he turned to song;
The mighty grief of rivers and of woods
Changed at his tread to noble scorn of death;
The clouded sun he bade break forth and flame
A dazzling splendor down the track of doom.
Then, as one leaving some delightful spot
On which he should not look again, turned round,
And, flashing farewells from his eyes across
The fading world, stood face to face with Death.
And he, beholding such a noble form,
Bowed low, and bade Time speak his latest wish,
And straightway granted it so soon as heard.
Then, like a Samson, Time went forth and felt
The solid pillars of the universe;

And, ere Death was aware of his design,
They bowed, brake, and thundered ruin upon ruin,
Realm on realm, one awful avalanche of
Flaming worlds, leaping to fathomless deeps,
Where Time and Death lay side by side,—
  uncrowned.

U. S. A.—1873.

A STORY, by my guardian-angel told,
Through the low breathings of a weary night.

  In this fair realm, washed by four rolling
    seas,
There are who plunder what they should protect;
And with the stolen keys of law, unlock
To shameless shame the people's hard-earned
    store,
Laid by to rule becoming a fair name.
What record tells a crime of deeper dye
Than that a man should rob his country to
Her face; then mock her rising voice of scorn?
Ill fares that realm which cannot trust her own!
Shorn of her strength by those she had made
    strong;
Finding her sons what foes would blush to be.
But clothed in wrath she will arise and smite
With the dread weapon of a people's will.

  I saw grand temples, where gay Fashion sits,
A seventh-day patron of high God, all jewelled,
Ringed, and covered with gay plumage, nodding

To the drowsy drone of classic periods,
Shaping a Christ to please the reigning mood;
While Prayer, aghast, sinks on the altar stairs,
And Reverence flies, amazed to see the forms
Which at the footlights stood but yesternight,
Rise up to chant a solemn praise to God.
If He who came so poor should come again,
At the world's inn he still would find no room.

    Honesty I saw walk barefoot through the
Streets; and Fraud drive, clad in purple, to a
Golden throne, whose brightness blinded Justice;
While Guilt, in Virtue's garb, laughed loud to hear
Through a faint blame the undertone of praise.
Judges there were who judged unrighteously,
And sheathed the sword which should have hewn
      in twain
The Agags of iniquity, nor spared
The bleating spoil till wrathful Samuel comes.

    A nation mother I beheld press a
Dread cup to her own children's lips, the blight
Whereof did palsy mighty limbs, and shake
With staggering fiends the bases of her strength.
Mammon I saw build stately halls on sand,
By treacherous seas of speculation; and
The floods came, the winds beat, and with a crash
That shook a nation pale, they fell and passed.

    These are but the pangs of Time in travail;
The infant cry of a pure age I hear,
Wherein a tongue of fire shall smite the brow
Of sin, proclaim the Christ, uprear the cross,
And crush with light the darkness of the world.

DAY.

What! ho, bright Day! how many times hast run
In hot haste round this weary world; leaping
The rivers, dashing o'er voiceless wastes, hills;
Skipping from shore to shore, from pole to pole;
Flashing the light of thy bright eyes on hut,
Prison, palace, temple, mart; climbing the
Icy glaciers of the north, and breasting
The balmy breezes of the south; striving
To keep the weary world awake, with Night
Close at thy heels to undo all thou'st done,
And hide the impress of thy golden feet?
What! ho, there! gone so soon? I never saw
A fellow with so strong a will to do
The thing he set his mind on: kings cannot
Change his purpose, nor armies beat him back.
He will, for pastime, kick a crown down thro'
A realm; make, break, decree, revoke, build and
Destroy at pleasure. Now he decks a brow
With flowers, then turns and withers all the bloom.
Fond he is, and fickle as a child; a
Thief he is that steals away our life; a
Friend who helps us to the goal; a despot,
Crushing whom he will; yet, so kind withal,
The children love him, the glad flowers greet him;
All joyous things in heaven and earth list for
His step, and weep when he is gone. Strange
    moods
He hath, and ways: some he wakes to sorrow,
Some to joy, yet smiles as sweetly on the
Peasant as the prince, and sits as much at

Home in lowly cot as lordly hall, nor
Scorns one board, however humbly spread.
Now, as an artist, he will paint for fame;
Then, like a spiteful critic, daub it out.
Anon with harp on mountain top he weaves
Sweet melodies, then madly breaks the strings,
And moves, a songless bard, where once he sang.
In sullen moods he will make quarrel with
The earth, and smite her brow with savage storms;
Then, vexed with his own rudeness, make amends,
Kiss her with sunshine and heal all her wounds.

NIGHT.

 She walks in solemn pomp amid the stars;
Her darkly-flowing tresses wet with dew,
And all her gloom-fringed garments sweeping aisles
Eternity hath trod to her high shrines.

 She is Time's ministering angel, pouring
Sweet balm into his wounded heart; encircling
All his weary way and waning life with
The broad compass of a mother's love, from
Whose dark womb he came, a child of light, to
Struggle with innumerable ills and die
A lonely death, deserted by his own.
And when the prodigal hours have claimed
Their portion, and to the far country fled,
Making a childless waste of his fair realm,
She stays his heart on a strong psalm of trust,
Till other children speak and bear his name.

Upon Toil's thundering wheel she lays her
Hand, and holds in restful pause a weary world.
The wounded heart, touching her garment's hem,
Is healed; and Sorrow, beholding her calm
Face, forgets to weep. A kindly gloom she
Folds around pale Thought; lest, worn with gazing
Long upon unfathomable deeps, he
Fall from his high throne, blinded with light.
At her approach Care lays his burden down,
And rests his brow on that which seam'd it o'er;
The slave forgets his chain, the king his crown,
And Poverty that ever she was poor.
Pain flies the wound, and Fear lays by the goad;
The homeless wanderer dreams he is at home,
And hears his mother speak a changeless love.
The sailor-boy, in his rude hammock swung,
Greets the one face he thought so fair at school,
And where the din of battle lately rolled
The soldier sleeps in blood beside the slain.
O'er million-peopled cities, hamlets lone;
On mighty woods, where song rolls her full tide,
And up the dusty highways of the world,
The soothing shadow of her presence falls.
A stillness, solemn, dread; a calm, serene
And blest; a gift God's own belovèd share,
Comes down from heaven to earth where'er she
    moves.
Unnumbered weary brows she kindly decks
With crowns of rest and chaplets of repose,
Breathing a sweet evangel of God's love
From the deep purpose of perpetual change.
So o'er the troubled sea of life she walks,
Whispering peace, and all the waves grow still.

JESUS OF NAZARETH PASSES BY.

Bring into the way all the halt and blind,
The diseased in soul, the troubled in mind;
The hearts that are burdened with sin and care,
The weakened in faith, the feeble in prayer,
And blossoms of promise that sicken to die,
For Jesus of Nazareth passes by.

Bring down from the darkened chambers of doubt,
All the bridegroom lamps, with their lights gone
    out,
The talents you find under napkins hid,
The moth-eaten garments of guests who're bid
To the marriage feast when Time shall die,
For Jesus of Nazareth passes by.

Bring out from the charnel-house of Despair
All the whitened bones that lie mouldering there,
All the folded hands on the King's highway
That will not work for a penny a day,
With hearts that wither and know not why,
For Jesus of Nazareth passes by.

He is passing now! Oh, touch but the hem
Of his flowing robes, there's virtue in them.
He speaks but the word, and the sobbings cease,
"Thy sins be forgiven thee, go in peace,"
And onward up Calvary's hill to die,
Jesus of Nazareth passes by.

THE MINISTRY OF ANGELS.

Waiting to fly for the King,
  Waiting to hear him say,
Speed on thy swiftest wing,
  Help the fainting to pray,
  Teach the weary to sing.
To be doing is to choose higher walks and farther
    seeing,
To be idle is to lose half the blessedness of being.

Some are striving with the erring,
  Fallen by the way,
By their loving whispers stirring
  Hopes that crowned a nobler day,
Till the prodigal weeps, hearing
  His old mother for him pray.

Where hunger pinches
  Day after day,
Where death by inches
  Tears life away;
Where the hopes wither,
  And the joys die,
Thither, oh, thither,
  God's angels fly.

To back streets where never preacher
  Thinks 'twill pay to bend a knee,
God sends down a noble teacher
  From his higher ministry.

Where eyes worn with pious weeping,
    Dare not look lest sin should blight,
God sends holy angels keeping
    Loving watches day and night.

In God's plan no mind, observing,
    Findeth either great or small;
All the angels feel in serving
    Is that Jesus died for all.

Some fly to the weeping
    With eyes fixed on the wall;
Some watch o'er the sleeping,
    That David smite not Saul;
While God himself is keeping
    High watches over all.

Under the deep blue sea, closing lips of the drowned:
In through the palace gates teaching the newly crowned.
    Sword can never shield a nation,
        Art nor science, sermon, song;
    Nor the strength of education
        Crush the curse that follows wrong;
    His pure laws who wrought salvation,
        Only maketh nations strong.

In through the prison cell,
    In through the halls of state,
In where the white lips tell
    Some one is desolate;
Any where, but in hell,
    The angels labor and wait.

LIGHTENED BY LOOKING.

"*They looked unto him and were lightened.*"

As at morn the upturned face
Feels the sun's inspiring rays,
Wears the glory and the glow
Crowning all the world below,
So Christ melts the shadows dim
From the eye that looks on him.

When his glory faintly flamed,
Prophets looked, were not ashamed,
And with lightened faces saw
Jesus shining through the law,
While faith saving trust did yield
To a love but half revealed.

Now the cross is lifted high,
Look and live: why will ye die?
Dawn which cheered the prophets' way
Melts into the perfect day:
Life for look doth Jesus give,
All the world may look and live.

Look, all ye by guilt opprest!
Ye who weary seek for rest!
Smoking flax nor bruisèd rush,
Christ will neither quench nor crush,
But redeem from sin and death
All who look on him by faith.

LANGUAGE OF DAYS.

"Days should speak."

Days should speak, and days should tell
    Wisdom deep in rapid flight:
"Use us wisely, use us well,
    Swiftly comes the solemn night."

Days should speak, and as they fly
    O'er the toiler and the tomb:
"Lo! the end of time is nigh,
    With the thunder crash of doom."

Days should speak with voice of love
    To the mourner 'neath the rod:
"There is rest for thee above,
    In the paradise of God."

Days should speak, and speaking break
    All the bands of them that sleep:
"To yon fields, awake, awake!
    For the Master comes to reap."

Days should speak by setting suns,
    Fading noon and fleeting hours,
And that stream of death which runs
    Through the cities and the flowers.

Days should speak, are speaking now,
    Language plain to you and me:
"There is falling on Time's brow
    Shadows of eternity."

WHAT OF THE NIGHT?

Watchman, oh! what of this dark night of Time?
Canst see through the light of the stars that shine,
A coming of shadows and darkness deep,
When the saved shall sing and the lost shall weep?
Canst hear the sound of the archangel's tread
As he comes to waken the pious dead?

I can see the shadows on Time's worn dial,
'Twill darken its face in a little while;
I can hear the voice of the Master say,
"Behold, I come quickly!" he may come to-day;
But the hour I know not, nor they who wait
For the Bridegroom to pass the pearly gate.

Oh! why should you question about the night?
Your garments are stained; go, wash them white;
Let your lamps be trimmed, your vessels o'erflow,
For you cannot buy oil in the night, you know.
Should darkness come on, and you lose your way,
You never can reach the portals of day.

Watchman, oh! what of this dark night of sin?
Will the clouds never break, and the light roll in?
Shall the glorious cross but bless a part
Of the world now cursed with a sinful heart?
Shall a cleansing fountain be opened wide,
And only a few step into its tide?

The morning cometh, a glorious day,
When the clouds of sin shall vanish away;
The nations now sitting in darkness and night
Shall hear of its brightness and press to its light;
The knowledge of Jesus with blood-waves sweep,
And cover the earth as waters the deep.

O watchman! come tell us of death's dark night:
Will the sightless eyes never see the light?
Will the lips that closed with a cry of pain
Never speak to the long lost love again?
And the hands now folded in dreamless rest
Never feel their grasp who have loved them best?

Oh, glorious thought! the morning will come
When the lips shall sing that are now so dumb,
And the pale hands folded o'er hearts so dead
Fling back the folds of their clay-wrought bed;
And the feet so weary when earth was trod
Shall walk in the weariless land of God.

AND YET THERE IS ROOM.

Oh! come, heavy-laden, distressed,
   And come whosoever will,
At Calvary's haven of rest
   There is room for sinners still.

Oh! spread the glad tidings abroad,
   Where the sun shall rise and set:
There is room in the love of God
   For every poor sinner yet.

For those who have wandered away,
  For those who have long delayed,
There is room, there is room to-day,
  At the feast which Christ hath made.

Oh! sorrowful, wearied, and poor;
  Oh! stained and burdened by sin:
Why linger so long at the door?
  There is room, there is room: come in!

WHAT WILT THOU DO IN THE SWELLING OF JORDAN?

What wilt thou do when the moan
  Of Jordan round thee rolls,
Waiting to drift all alone
  Into the land of souls?
No Jesus to guide thee on,
  Through gloom and painful strife,
Far into the peaceful dawn
  Of everlasting life!

What wilt thou do when the beat
  Of heart is sad and slow,
And the cold waves round thy feet
  Come with a swifter flow?
No pillar to lean upon
  Wrought out by faith and prayer,
The sunlight of hope all gone,
  And Jesus is not there!

RARE KNOWLEDGE.

"Thou hast known my soul in adversity."

False is every wind that bloweth;
  Tears can smile of friendship dim;
In adversity God knoweth
  Every heart that trusts in him.

In prosperity we borrow
  Smile from all whom aid we lend;
It is in the hour of sorrow
  God comes down to be our friend.

When we fall by sudden sinning,
  And the vultures sweep in sight,
Comes the voice of mercy winning
  Us again to truth and right.

Though the plans we laid deceive us,
  And all trusted friends depart,
God will never, never leave us
  If his love is in our heart.

THE TESTIMONY.

"I will declare what he hath done for my soul."

O Soul! what hath the Saviour wrought?
  Be now thy lips unsealed!
It passeth all the bounds of thought,
  Though only half revealed.

The prison and the chains are gone,
    The night has fled away,
And I behold the purple dawn
    Of everlasting day.

A new light floods the heart and mind,
    Whatever it may be:
I only know I once was blind,
    But now can plainly see.

My life from out the lowest dust,
    A Saviour's hand did raise;
And in that Saviour now I trust
    And sing that Saviour's praise.

PATIENT WAITING.

"Rest in the Lord, and wait patiently for him."

Rest in the Lord, and wait his time,
With patient hope, and trust sublime:
A thousand years do pass away,
And seem to him but as one day.

Rest in the Lord, a pathway bright
He opens through the darkest night,
And patient hope beholds the dawn
Of morning ere the night is gone.

Rest in the Lord all ye who bear
The burdens of depressing care,
And eyes with weeping long grown dim,
Rest, and wait patiently for him.

Rest in the Lord: his plans, though vast,
Will all be brought to light at last,
And things now lost in shadows dread
Will everlasting glories shed.

WRATH OF GOD AND THE LAMB.

Oh the wrath of God and the Lamb!
  Who can bear the terrible weight?
For the pity of Love it doth damn
  Far more than the scorn of a hate.
Send the blight of a fiery rain,
  Send the numbing breath of the frost:
It were lighter far than the pain
  Of knowing that heaven is lost.

Oh the sight of a wounded hand!
  The ringing of heavenly bells,
It illumines a godless land
  With the glare of a thousand hells.
Could the eye of memory close,
  Or the lips of the past grow dumb,
Then the devil would find repose
  In the gloom of the years to come.

No hell, did the moralist say,
  No hate in a merciful God?
Come flame-waves, and dash me away
  From a wounded Christ for a rod.
Oh! is there no ocean of flame,
  No tempest of fire from above,
To shield from the terrible shame
  Of hating an infinite Love?

No cavern where spirit may hide
  From the glance of merciful eyes,
The rebuke of a wounded side,
  And the music of paradise?
Fierce burning would be more a dove-
  Like token of heavenly fate,
Than to feel that God is all love
  Ruling over a heart of hate.

IMMORTALITY OF THE SOUL.

The dust returns to earth again,
  The soul to God on high;
Though suns may set and moons may wane,
  A spirit cannot die.

When death-knell of the rolling years
  By worlds on fire is rung,
And all that's mortal disappears,
  The soul will still be young.

Its springs of life from God arise,—
  Oh soul-refreshing truth!
Eternity alone supplies
  The measure of its youth.

www.ingramcontent.com/pod-product-compliance
Lightning Source LLC
Chambersburg PA
CBHW020910230426
43666CB00008B/1397